FLOWERING
VINES

D1414831

Beautiful
Climbers

Karan Davis Cutler-Guest Editor

Janet Marinelli
SERIES EDITOR

Jane Ludlam
MANAGING EDITOR

Bekka Lindstrom
ART DIRECTOR

Stephen K-M. Tim
VICE PRESIDENT, SCIENCE, LIBRARY & PUBLICATIONS

Judith D. Zuk
PRESIDENT

Elizabeth Scholtz
DIRECTOR EMERITUS

Handbook #158

Copyright © Spring 1999 by the Brooklyn Botanic Garden, Inc.

Handbooks in the *21st-Century Gardening Series,* formerly *Plants & Gardens,*
are published quarterly at 1000 Washington Ave., Brooklyn, NY 11225.

Subscription included in Brooklyn Botanic Garden subscriber membership dues ($35.00 per year).

ISSN # 0362-5850   ISBN # 1-889538-10-8

Printed by Science Press, a division of the Mack Printing Group

TABLE OF CONTENTS

FLOWERING VINES 101

by Karan Davis Cutler

NORTH AMERICA IS THE HOME of horizontal gardeners. Not gardeners who work flat on their backs—or spend all their time in chaise lounges—but gardeners whose vision is earthbound. A few trees and shrubs may creep into our landscapes, but our sight usually is directed down and straight ahead, making it easy for us to forget plants that grow up rather than hug the ground. Making it easy to forget flowering vines.

Gardeners in other parts of the world aren't so myopic. They use vines with abandon: to creep along the tops of walls, twine up pillars and posts, bestride gateways, blanket fences, roof arbors, and shade patios. The British, in particular, are besotted by flowering vines, so much so that any Guernsey that loiters over a patch of clover is in danger of being planted with the clematis 'Lady Betty Balfour'. Americans, always conscious of English horticultural imperialism, would do well to take this page from their garden book.

Climbers, after all, were among the first cultivated plants. Egyptian wall paintings (c. 1400 B.C.) show slaves harvesting fruit from vine-covered pergolas, and the Romans used roses, ivy, and other climbers to gar-

To transform an ordinary wall into a thing of beauty, a flowering vine like this sweet pea needs only some string to cling to as it climbs toward the sun.

Some vines use twining tendrils to climb.

land and shade. The grape was so common in ancient agriculture that it is referred to only as "the vine" in the Bible, and rare was the medieval garden whose walls weren't home to climbing plants.

UPWARD MOBILITY

Likely it was the limits of the natural world—space, climate, water, soil, light, and competition with other plants—that gave rise to vines in the first place. Rather than a distinct botanical category, like monocotyledons or magnolias, vines are a behavioral group, plants that adapted to their surroundings by becoming scandent. In order to move water and food easily from their roots to their leaves, they developed hollow stems.

Many true vines are tropical plants, natives of regions where the mercury stays well above 32°F. In such warm climates, the fluids moving through a vine's long, hollow stems—sometimes dozens and dozens of feet long—never freeze, a process as destructive to a vine as it is to the water pipes in your home.

Some scientists believe that the climbing response of vines also is a reaction to threats. Like plants that developed thorns to protect their fruits from being eaten by animals, vines may have stretched the distance between nodes (the points on the stem where leaves form) in order to move their fruits out of the reach of predators. Or to make their flowers more accessible to the birds and insects that pollinate them.

A derelict tractor becomes a picturesque support for a Virginia creeper vine.

Whatever the selective pressures, the adaptive behavior of vining species was fodder for Charles Darwin, who was always on the prowl for examples of the natural battle for survival. In 1865, Darwin published "The Movements and Habits of Climbing Plants" in the *Journal of the Linnaean Society*, an essay he expanded into a 200-page book two decades later. His argument was that plants evolved into climbers because of competition: "Plants become climbers, in order, as it may be presumed, to reach the light and to expose a large surface of their leaves to its action and to that of the free air."

Giving up sleep for several nights to watch a *Ceropegia*, Darwin recorded its attempts to find something to help it climb. Its movements, he wrote, seemed so purposeful that it appeared as if the plant could think. "It was an interesting spectacle to watch the long shoot sweeping this grand circle, night and day, in search of some object round which to twine."

The elliptical motion of twining plants, called "circumnutation" by botanists, can be clockwise or counterclockwise, depending on the

FAUX VINES

Espaliers are another group of "climbing" plants—or, more accurately, plants that have been trained to flatten themselves against walls, trellises, and other vertical surfaces. The word *espalier*, from the Italian *spalle*, or shoulder, once referred solely to the method; today the term is used to describe both the method and the plant.

Pears and apples are the quintessential plants that are pruned and trained into the set patterns of espalier—palmette verriers, vertical cordons, and more—but the practice doesn't stop with fruit trees. Pyracanthas, forsythias, and magnolias are only three of the many ornamentals coaxed into botanical bondage, as one wag termed the practice.

Artificial but stunning, espalier transforms shrubs and trees into vines—an endorsement of the value of climbers in gardens if ever there were one.

species. The direction is typically at a right angle to the source of light or heat, and twining plants, if turned upside down, will uncoil and recircle their support. Guide a twiner in the "wrong" direction—American bittersweet, for instance, circles clockwise—and the plant will rewind itself. Similarly, a vine that is pulled away from its support will reseek it. Interestingly, the higher a twiner grows, the more tightly it clasps its support.

UP, UP, AND AWAY

Not all scandent plants are twiners, however. Botanists have identified more than two dozen specific ways that plants climb, but most are variations of five basic techniques.
- Vines that weave or twine, such as mandevillas
- Vines that attach with aerial roots or adhesive pads, such as climbing hydrangea
- Vines that scramble, such as potato vine
- Vines that catch with thorns, such as bougainvilleas
- Vines that clasp with tendrils or petioles, such as sweet pea

Most commonly grown vines either twine around vertical structures or

Many ornamental shrubs or trees that are not vines, such as this 'Golden Delicious' apple, can be trained as espaliers to form a pattern against a wall or trellis.

adhere to vertical surfaces. The differences in how vines climb are important to gardeners because they guide us on how to guide them. For example, no golden-trumpet vine is going to climb a bare wall, as trumpet vine will. Golden-trumpet vine needs a support around which to twine—and tying to get started.

One job of gardeners is to provide appropriate climbing apparatuses—horticultural jungle gyms—for their vines. This chore also creates an opportunity to add an attractive built element to the landscape, such as a rail fence, a lamp pole, a stone wall, a graceful archway, a wrought-iron trellis, or a classic arbor. You should look for a support that meshes with the style of your house or garden, but anything can serve to support a vine. Not long ago on a trip to the Midwest to see my daughter, I came across an abandoned John Deere tractor, which had found a second career as the underpinning for a volunteer Virginia creeper. Fortunately, from my husband's point of view, the tractor was not for sale.

KEEPING THE LID ON

While most vines are like two-year-old children—who are frequently heard to announce, "I do it myself!"—not every climber heads skyward at lightning speed. Some species take their time even to get started. Climbing hydrangea is a good example; as one mail-order house diplomatically phrased it, climbing hydrangea "is a bit slow to establish itself." Mine took a half-dozen years. Other vines just grow slowly, a trait that can be a virtue if you have a small garden or are cultivating climbers in containers.

Many species need a hand—either a hand up or a heavy hand. Securing and guiding will help almost any climber, at least at the start of its journey, and pruning not only keeps plants in bounds but will improve their form and promote flowering. Guidelines on when to prune, which are based on when vines bloom, are covered in "Growing Vines Successfully" (page 29).

But the most important key to growing vines successfully is location. Most problems can be avoided if you choose an appropriate site for the plant. That means full sun for a vine that craves it, protection from the wind for a vine that needs it, and plenty of water for a vine that demands it. A strong, vigorous plant is unlikely to become a victim of diseases or pests. Happily, most flowering vines are rarely touched by the fungal, bacterial, and viral diseases that plague other plants in the garden.

In fact, nearly all of the news about flowering vines is happy. They are an independent and wonderfully vigorous crew. The following chapters

Pruning and guiding give a boost to blossoming climbers such as this clematis and 'Phyllis Bide' rose, springing from a bed of 'Hidcote' lavender.

are intended to help you grow them successfully, as well as to introduce some names that may be unknown to you. Plant something new, by all means, but don't turn your back on the familiar simply because it *is* familiar. Some of the best known vines are also the best performers, tried-and-true plants guaranteed to do well in a variety of settings. As Connecticut garden writer Sydney Eddison observed, "The perfect plant is the one that's alive."

CHAPTER TWO

USING VINES IN THE GARDEN

by Kathleen Fisher

AFTER YEARS AWAY from the Deep South, the garden writer Henry Mitchell wrote, "I have given up thinking of coral vines, fat gardenia bushes, and much else, but I have not given up the notion that a garden should have a lot of leaves in it, preferably hanging from the air . . . ." Not content with foliage alone, Mitchell set roses twining about his entryway and into the canopy of his trees. He allowed grapes and clematis to scramble over his simple summer house and coaxed a borderline-hardy creeping fig to grow up the sides of his raised pool.

It's often said that vines are the best friends of a passionate gardener with a small urban lot like Mitchell's. And it's true: There's no better way to splash color and texture around a postage-stamp property than by collecting plants that grow skyward rather than sideways. But this doesn't begin to give vines their due, for there are no more versatile creatures in plantdom.

Take a setting different from Mitchell's, one of today's treeless suburban mini-estates. For fast relief, owners can create garden rooms with inexpensive trellises and festoon them with climbers. Vines clambering

Splash color and texture on garden objects with vines such as native honeysuckle.

VINE VILLAINS

Just as one gardener's weed is another gardener's flower, a vine can be perfectly well behaved in one region and horribly invasive somewhere else. Given the right conditions, these vines can take over. Before you plant one of them, check with botanical gardens or local nature preserve managers.

Brazilian jasmine (*Jasminum dichotomum*)
Chinese wisteria (*Wisteria sinensis*)
English ivy (*Hedera helix*)
German ivy (*Delairea odorata*)
Gold Coast jasmine (*Jasminum azoricum*)
Japanese honeysuckle (*Lonicera japonica*)
Kudzu (*Pueraria lobata*)
Oriental bittersweet (*Celastrus orbiculatus*)
Porcelain berry (*Ampelopsis brevipedunculata*)
Mile-a-minute vine (*Polygonum perfoliatum*)
Moonseed (*Menispermum canadense*)
Periwinkle (*Vinca major*)
Wood rose (*Merremia tuberosa*)

Avoid planting invasive vines like this Oriental bittersweet.

up the house itself will quickly create the illusion that the structure is part of its setting, rather than an intruder. And if you're an apartment dweller with nary a scrap of land, you can still grow vines, either in containers outdoors—wrap them along your balcony railing—or indoors in a sunny window.

USING VINES ON STRUCTURES

Excuses for buying vines are many. We all have drab structures that could use some pizzazz—a chain link fence, a tree stump, the broad side of a barn. Camouflage is a use that's invariably suggested for vines. If you have a truly hideous structure, though, keep in mind that in temperate North America a flowering vine is rarely a year-round solution, since few are reliably evergreen. More accurate words than *camouflage* for what vines will accomplish on structures include *softening* (against something cold, such as a concrete wall), *enhancing* (against something serviceable but plain, such as a split-rail fence), or *distracting* (on something that could use repair but isn't ready to fall down, such as the storage shed in my yard).

Vines can also serve as co-conspirators for screening when coupled with a supporting structure. An especially useful place for them is the area garden designers call the utility, or service, area (the rest of us call it the trash-can area). Near a seating area, a vine-trellis duo will help you block too-brisk breezes.

Children enjoy rustic teepees set in the garden and covered with vines such as hyacinth bean.

AUTUMN BEAUTIES

A few flowering vines also have brilliantly hued leaves in autumn or colorful fruits or seed pods, providing a second season of color. Among the best are these:

American bittersweet (*Celastrus scandens*), fruits
Boston ivy (*Parthenocissus tricuspidata*), foliage
Bottle gourd (*Lagenaria siceraria*), fruits
Grapes (*Vitis* species), foliage & fruits
Hyacinth bean (*Lablab purpureus*), fruits
Honeysuckles (*Lonicera* species), fruits
Roses (*Rosa* species), fruits
Scarlet runner bean (*Phaseolus coccineus*), fruits
Silver vine (*Actinidia polygama*), fruits
Snake gourd (*Trichosanthes cucumerina*), fruits
Virginia creeper (*Parthenocissus quinquefolia*), foliage

If your support already exists, it will dictate to some extent the vines you choose. Those lucky enough to have stone or brick walls or fences can grow brawny vines like climbing hydrangea, which doesn't even need help in climbing. The woody trunk and stems of wisterias will become similarly gnarly and eye-catching with age, although they need strict discipline.

At the other end of the support spectrum is a leaning wooden fence like our neighbors'. Fortunately, there are plenty of featherweight vines, especially among annual species. Cypress vine is one of my favorites. Lightweight climbers can be grown on netting and strings as well as unsturdy fences.

VINES OVERHEAD

Arbors and pergolas—despite neglectful owners who sometimes allow them to appear naked in public—were invented to be clothed in vines. On a large property they can provide a womblike enclosure. In a small garden, they make a viewer feel there's more going on than meets the eye, both overhead and beyond the leafy walls.

In an area where you'll often sit to relax or dine, it's an added bonus if flowers hang overhead or send their fragrance swirling through your

FRAGRANT CLIMBERS

Carolina jessamine (*Gelsemium sempervirens*)
Chilean jasmine (*Mandevilla laxa*)
Clematis (*Clematis armandii, C. montana, C. recta*)
Climbing roses (*Rosa* species and cultivars)
Confederate jasmine (*Trachelospermum jasminoides*)
Cup and saucer vine (*Cobaea scandens*)
Dutchman's pipe (*Aristolochia macrophylla*)
Five-leaf akebia (*Akebia quinata*)
Frost grape (*Vitis riparia*)
Honeysuckles (*Lonicera* species)
Jasmines (*Jasminum* species)
Madagascar jasmine (*Stephanotis floribunda*)
Moonflower (*Ipomoea alba*)
Silver vines (*Actinidia* species)
Sweet pea (*Lathyrus odoratus*)
Wisterias (*Wisteria* species)

shady bower. But remember that all that nectar will attract bees. If you think that will spoil your party, keep your "ceiling" high overhead.

Arches are another piece of garden furniture often misused, plopped in the middle of a lawn like a door leading from nowhere to nowhere. Placed to mark the transition between two garden areas, or on a path, however, a vine-draped arch can practically make cymbals crash.

THE SKY'S THE LIMIT

You don't need elaborate structures to grow vines, though. A simple post in the midst of a perennial border will give you a place to train a clematis for a strong, vertical line. If you really want to express yourself, you can become as fanciful as you like, training your vines into ladders, scallops, or curlicues against a fence or wall. Or train a vine along a rope, wire, or chain swag, giving your garden a theatrical atmosphere. Just as vines may be used for camouflage, they can also be trained to highlight an architectural feature, like a pointing finger. Use vines to accentuate the edge of a deck or steps, or wrap one around the pedestal of a garden statue or birdbath.

EDIBLE CLIMBERS & RAMBLERS

Bottle gourd (*Lagenaria siceraria*)
Cucumber (*Cucumis sativus*)
Grapes (*Vitis* species)
Hop (*Humulus lupulus*)
Hyacinth bean (*Lablab purpureus*)
Kiwi (*Actinidia deliciosa*)
Melon (*Cucumis melo*)
Passion flowers (*Passiflora* species)
Pea (*Pisum sativum*)
Pole bean (*Phaseolus vulgaris*)
Pumpkins (*Cucurbita* species)
Scarlet runner bean (*Phaseolus coccineus*)

Straight branches an inch or so in diameter, or bamboo, which our area has in unfortunate abundance, provide free material for building rustic teepees where vines can clamber in the midst of a vegetable plot or cottage garden. Children love hideaways and won't be able to resist a teepee smothered in scarlet runner beans, hyacinth beans, morning glories, or all three.

VINE VERSATILITY

Vines are justifiably honored for the wonderful way they mingle with other plants, climbing either on them or with them. You can send climbing hydrangeas or roses shooting up a tree, or weave them through each other. Roses and clematis are a classic combination. You can use a bright-flowering vine like climbing nasturtium to light up an evergreen or give a spring-blooming shrub a summer color boost. Alternatively, choose a vine and supporting shrub or tree that bloom at the same time.

If you garden to attract wildlife, some vines are a must because of their nectar or berries. For example, passion flowers are a larval food for various butterfly species. Or define the edge of your "bird garden" with a trellis of trumpet vine or native honeysuckle (*Lonicera sempervirens*); both are magnets for hummingbirds, and the latter can eventually create a tangle of woody stems where birds can hide from predators or build a nest.

When fragrance is the goal, consider your daily routine. If you don't have time to stop and smell the roses, it may be enough to plant them

A fast-growing flowering vine such as hyacinth bean (*Lablab purpureus*) makes a colorful backdrop to a vegetable patch as it scrambles up a fence.

around your front door, where you can catch a whiff as you dash to work. But what about stationing them off the back patio instead, where you occasionally unwind with a novel or cold beverage? When planting for fragrance, keep in mind prevailing breezes and situate your aromatic vines upwind.

You also can discover entire new worlds of scent with tender vines that are often cultivated indoors, such as hoyas and jasmines, trained up posts or mini-trellises, or around windows. Indoors or out, don't be afraid to try a vine in a container—within reason. Not surprisingly, container-growing works better with species that grow to 8' than with those that grow to 30'. Still, moderately vigorous vines that are on the borderline for pot living can be kept happy with regular and severe pruning. Horticultural tough love.

A vine that is allowed to grow downward can look like a floral waterfall. Elevate it in a container high overhead.

A number of vines and viny creepers, such as periwinkle (*Vinca major*), are often recommended as groundcovers. Remember that the term groundcover is used loosely. If you've planted a vine as a groundcover, the term means, "if you plant it, you won't be able to see the ground" rather than, "you can walk on it like turf." The Ipswich, Massachusetts, specialty nursery Completely Clematis recommends *Clematis viticella* 'Madame

VINES FOR WILDLIFE

These vines provide food, shelter—or both—for birds. To grow a birdhouse, try planting bottle gourds (*Lagenaria* species).

Alabama supplejack (*Berchemia scandens*)
American bittersweet (*Celastrus scandens*)
Cardinal climbers (*Ipomoea quamoclit* or *I.* × *multifida*)
Carolina moonseed (*Cocculus carolinus*)
Grapes (*Vitis* species)
Honeysuckles (*Lonicera* species)
Moonseed (*Menispermum canadense*)
Passionflowers (*Passiflora* species)
Sawbriers, greenbriers (*Smilax* species)
Trumpet creeper (*Campsis radicans*)
Virginia creeper (*Parthenocissus quinquefolia*)
Woodbine (*Parthenocissus inserta*)

Julia Correvon' as a groundcover, and no doubt other clematis could also be woven between plants in a perennial border. Virginia creeper (*Parthenocissus quinquefolia*) is a North American native vine sometimes used as a groundcover that also provides fall color before defoliating. A few of the traditional groundcover vines, like English ivy (*Hedera helix*), can easily become bullies. Talk to neighbors before you plant if you're unsure about which vines are invasive in your area. (See "Vine Villains," page 14).

A WORD OR TWO OF CAUTION

When I asked a somewhat cynical friend for the first thing that popped into his head on hearing the word *vine*, his response was true to form: "Overgrown." The fact is that the amenable, quick-growing nature of vines can sometimes spell trouble, from requiring a bit more maintenance than you might like, to ruining your relationship with the neighbors, to gobbling up acres of countryside and causing serious ecological damage.

Think about the eventual height and spread of your vine before you plant. How much time do you want to spend on a ladder to keep your vine from blocking a window? If you have a two-story house, high-flying vines

Many vines, such as trumpet creeper, attract birds and other wildlife to backyards.

such as Dutchman's pipe will rightly tempt you. But if you have a ranch-style house, choose species that stay under 10', or plan to spend time training your vines toward the horizontal.

The old warnings about ivy destroying brickwork are unfounded if your mortar is in good shape. But a frisky young wisteria can wreak havoc with drainpipes and gutters, and any vigorous vine is an ill-chosen companion for wooden shingles. An enthusiastic climbing rose like 'New Dawn' will put a flimsy trellis to an acid test if you miss a season of pruning.

These are relatively minor annoyances. Some vines, in the wrong home, are environmental nightmares, like pit bulls set loose in a preschool. Japanese honeysuckle can pull good-sized saplings to the ground; English ivy can weigh down branches of mature trees. Either plant will solidly blanket a forest floor, wiping out native wildflowers.

In short, as in any gardening, do your homework and choose a vine that's not only appropriate for your growing conditions and your garden but also for your energy level. After all, the goal is to create an inviting and relaxing retreat, not to spend your weekends patrolling your eaves with loppers, or your perimeter with a blow torch and a vat of herbicide.

CHAPTER THREE

GROWING VINES SUCCESSFULLY

by Andrew Bunting

VINES ARE A DIVERSE GROUP of plants. Most are easy to grow and require little care; however, a basic knowledge of their cultural needs is important for success in your garden.

If you're unfamiliar with the USDA Plant Hardiness Zone system, find out your zone from a local nursery. While you should take the USDA zone recommendations seriously, remember that location, like politics, is local. Within each USDA zone there are always microclimates that are warmer than the surrounding, larger region. But don't forget that a microclimate, especially one that is shady or exposed to wind, can also be colder than the encircling area.

Some of the most spectacular vines, such as bougainvillea and passion flower, are also tender—unable to tolerate cold temperatures. Because of their height, even hardy vines can't take full advantage of snow cover, as perennial flowers can. Attempting to sustain marginally hardy species of vines is an endless struggle. It's better to plant species that will thrive in your garden.

Make sure your vine gets all the sun or shade it needs. Full sun means at least 6 hours of direct sunlight daily.

SITE BASICS

In addition to matching a vine to its region, you must match it to its site. Light is a crucial element. Sun-demanding climbers, such as coral vine and roses, may survive in partial shade, but they won't thrive—and won't produce many flowers or fruits.

Make sure that your vine gets all the sun or shade it needs. When gardeners talk about full sun, they mean more than six hours of direct sunlight each day. A site in light shade gets some direct sun and some shade during the day, or bright, filtered light throughout the day. Full shade means no direct sunlight. Don't forget that some vines—silver lace vine

Golden-trumpet vine is easy to grow in a sunny spot or a perfectly drained pot.

is one—prefer full sun in northern regions but may want partial shade in hot parts of the country.

As a group, vines are vigorous growers and do best in organically rich soil. That doesn't mean heavily amending the planting hole: Recent research indicates that over-enriching a planting hole discourages roots from growing beyond the hole, slowing the plant's growth. Instead, turn over a shovelful of soil. If you find earthworms, the soil is in good shape. But if your soil contains a lot of sand or clay—or is seriously lacking in nutrients—you should improve it. In all cases, the solution is to add compost, composted manure, or other organic matter.

The great majority of vines aren't particular about soil pH. There are exceptions, however. Plant a wisteria in highly alkaline soil and its leaves turn yellow. If you have reason to think your planting site is extremely acidic or alkaline, do a pH test before you plant, and select a vine suited to the site.

PLANTING VINES

When to plant vines depends on where you live, what species of vine you've chosen, and whether your plant is container grown, bare-root, balled-and-burlapped (B&B), a small, tender transplant, or if you're beginning with seeds. The goal is to make sure that a good root system

FOUR SEASONS OF VINE WORK

Spring
- Prune vines that flower on this year's growth; remove any damaged or dead stems from all vines.
- Sow seeds of annual vines.
- Plant perennial vines in cold regions.
- Mulch and feed vines.
- Tie and train vines as needed.
- Take stem cuttings and/or layer stems.

Summer
- Prune vines that flower on old growth.
- Tie and train vines as needed.
- Make sure plants receive adequate water.
- Take stem cuttings and/or layer stems.

Fall
- Take stem cuttings and/or layer stems.
- Collect seeds.
- Plant perennial vines in warm regions.
- Clean up area around base of vines.
- Mulch vines for winter protection.

Winter
- Sow seeds of perennial and woody vines.
- Check that vines are secured to their supports.
- Prune hardiest vines that flower on new growth.

develops before the vine is stressed—by low temperatures in the North, or by high ones in the South. Bare-root vines should be planted at the same time as perennial flowers, shrubs, and trees—typically in spring in cold regions, or in autumn in warmer climates. Container-grown climbers can be set in the garden throughout the growing season, as long as you water them regularly (and provide shade, if necessary).

Dig a hole that is at least twice as wide as the root ball, but only one or two inches deeper. Gently remove a container plant from its pot (once out

DIRT POOR

The following vines are remarkably tolerant of poor soil:

American bittersweet (*Celastrus scandens)*
Dutchman's pipe (*Aristolochia macrophylla*)
Five-leaf akebia (*Akebia quinata*)
Flag-of-Spain (*Mina lobata*)
Japanese hydrangea vine (*Schizophragma hydrangeoides*)
Kiwis (*Actinidia* species)
Love-in-a-puff (*Cardiospermum halicacabum*)
Moonseed (*Menispermum canadense*)
Morning glories (*Ipomoea* species)
Nasturtiums (*Tropaeolum* species)
Silver lace vine (*Polygonum aubertii*)
Trumpet creeper (*Campsis radicans*)
Wisterias (*Wisteria* species)

of the container, handle the vine by the root ball), untangle any girdled roots, and place it in the hole. It should sit at the same level or very slightly higher than it was growing in the container (an exception is clematis; see page 40). Water the root ball generously, allow the water to drain, and then fill the hole with the soil you removed, tamping it firmly around the root ball. Cut back the plant to encourage branching, and finish the job by mulching with 1 or 2 inches of compost or other organic matter.

Handle B&B vines the same way. The traditional advice is to leave the burlap in place—removing any wires, cords, or other ties—but there is some evidence that roots develop more quickly if the cover is removed. Moreover, today's burlap may contain plastic threads, which will prevent the vine's roots from expanding. If removing the burlap is difficult, consider loosening it or slicing it several times with a knife after the root ball is in place.

Hardy bareroot vines should be planted as early in spring as the ground can be worked. Cut away any dead or broken roots, then soak the roots in water for 8 hours. Leave several inches of loosened soil in the bottom of the planting hole. Set the vine at the same level it was growing (the stem will be discolored, giving you a guideline), refill the hole with the soil you removed, and mulch.

Gardeners often start annual vines from seed indoors, then transplant them outside once the danger of frost has passed. If you've begun other annual plants, you know the regimen. Use a soilless mix to avoid "damping-off," a fungus that attacks seedlings. To speed germination, provide heat: Either place the planting container—a 3-inch pot is ideal—in a warm location, or set it on a heat mat or heat cables.

As soon as the seeds germinate, move their containers to a bright, airy, cool location. Water as needed, keeping the soil moist but not soggy, and feed every 10 days with a liquid organic fertilizer applied at half strength. If you've sown several seeds in one container, thin to one plant by cutting (not pulling) the ones you don't want.

Harden-off the seedlings two weeks before the expected transplant date by moving them outside to a sheltered location for a portion of each day. Leave them out a little longer each day, exposing them to increasing amounts of sun and wind, until they are fully acclimated to the outdoors. If you choose to purchase annual vines, they, too, should be hardened-off before they are planted in the ground.

Many annual vines, such as morning glories and sweet peas, grow rapidly enough that they can be sown outdoors. Follow the seed-packet directions, and remember that planting, transplanting, and setting-out time is also trellis time. Don't postpone installing any support your vine may need in order to climb—do it when you set out the plant.

Annual vines such as sweet peas can be sown directly outdoors after the danger of frost has passed.

Dutchman's pipe thrives on adversity: shade, ordinary soil, and a severe pruning.

MAINTAINING VINES

Food: Vines that are planted in fertile, organically rich soil and mulched once or twice a year with compost normally do not need to be fertilized (for information on the needs of clematis, see page 41, and roses, page 46). You can boost the growth of annual vines by feeding them twice during the growing season—once when they are about a foot tall and again when they begin to bud. In contrast, container-grown vines must be fertilized regularly.

Whatever the vine you're growing, be sure to use a balanced organic fertilizer, one in which the proportions of nitrogen, phosphorus, and potassium (the N-P-K numbers on the label) are equal. Avoid high-nitrogen fertilizers, which will produce lush foliage at the expense of flowers.

Water: While vines need good drainage—an important benefit of adding organic matter to the soil—most also require lots of moisture to support the heavy growth they make each year. Once climbers are well established, however, they rarely need watering unless they are growing in an exceptionally hot, windy location, or in sandy soil in a region that receives little rainfall. Wilting is an obvious sign that your vine needs to be watered—and that the soil in which it's growing needs more organic matter.

SHADE SURVIVORS

Gardens that lack sun don't have to lack vines. While almost no climbing plant thrives in darkness, these species do well in light shade.

American Bittersweet (*Celastrus scandens)*
Boston ivy, Virginia creeper, woodbine (*Parthenocissus* species)
Carolina jessamine (*Gelsemium sempervirens*)
Clematis (*Clematis macropetala, C. montana*)
Climbing hydrangea (*Hydrangea anomala* var. *petiolaris*)
Confederate or star jasmine (*Trachelospermum jasminoides*)
Cup and saucer vine (*Cobaea scandens*)
Dutchman's pipe (*Aristolochia macrophylla*)
Five-leaf akebia (*Akebia quinata*)
Grapes (*Vitis* species)
Honeysuckles (*Lonicera* species)
Japanese hydrangea vine (*Schizophragma hydrangeoides*)
Kiwis (*Actinidia* species)
Coral peas (*Hardenbergia* species)
Magnolia vine (*Schisandra chinensis*)
Moonseed (*Menispermum canadense*)
Orange clockvine (*Thunbergia gregorii*)
Pileostegia (*Pileostegia viburnoides*)
Silver lace vine (*Polygonum aubertii*)

Mulching will help retain moisture around the roots, as well as add nutrients to the soil.

Pruning: Many vines need selective pruning to keep them healthy and attractive—and in bounds! Begin the process when plants are small by pinching off stem tips to encourage branching. Always remove damaged,

THE KINDEST CUTS

Always use clean (rinse them in a bleach-water solution), sharp tools when pruning vines. To remove an entire stem, cut back to the base of the vine. To shorten a stem, cut back to above a bud. To encourage denser growth, cut above an inward-facing bud; to encourage open growth, cut above an outward-facing bud.

diseased, weak, and dead stems. It is also good to thin dense-growing or tangled vines: Allowing more air and sun to reach the plant discourages pests and disease.

Annual climbers need little cutting back, except for shaping, but gardeners often prune perennial species each year to encourage flowering and to keep them under control (for the special needs of clematis, see page 42, and roses, page 50). Perennial vines should be pruned on the same schedule as flowering shrubs:

• Climbers that bloom in spring on old wood (the buds are formed the previous summer), such as *Akebia quinata* and jasmines, should be pruned within a week or two after they blossom.

• Silver lace vine and others that bloom in late summer or fall on new growth should be pruned in late winter or early spring, before the flower buds form.

• Perennial climbers that die back completely—in contrast to just losing their leaves—in autumn should be cut off a few inches above the soil line and the dead growth removed.

Perennial vines that have gotten totally out of hand can be pruned severely. Some species, including coral vine, Dutchman's pipe, most honeysuckles, and black-eyed Susan vine, will tolerate being cut to the ground. Others will stand up better to being pruned in stages, over three or four years. Remove a portion of the vine's oldest stems each year, cutting them back to a foot above the ground. Rejuvenation pruning is best done is spring, at the same time new growth begins.

Pests & Diseases: Most vines are not bothered by pests and diseases. Rather than treat a problem, avoid trouble by keeping climbers healthy. Give plants the amount of light they prefer, don't crowd them, and don't over-fertilize. Keep the planting area clean: Pull weeds and remove debris. Don't prune when foliage is wet; use clean shears, loppers, and saws. Immediately remove any leaves, stems, and flowers that appear to

THE WAYS OF WISTERIA

Considerable pruning is required to keep wisteria blooming and in bounds. Although wisteria blooms in spring on old wood—which normally means pruning immediately after flowering—this vine should be cut back in summer.

Cut back the new shoots to the lower six buds (these small flowering branches are known as spurs), then prune again in late winter, cutting the previously pruned shoots back to three or four buds.

Many wisterias are grafted, so watch for shoots from the base of the plant, which come from the root. Remove them immediately, or the understock plant will overtake the wisteria growing above ground.

be diseased. Encourage beneficial wildlife—such as lady bird beetles and birds—to inhabit your garden.

When problems do occur, begin with the least toxic solution, such as hand-picking pests like Japanese beetles, hosing the vine with a sharp water spray, or treating with a dormant oil. Reserve botanical pesticides for the most serious problems, remembering that although these remedies are organic, they are poisons. (For specific problems and remedies, see "Clematis: The Queen of Vines," page 43; "Climbing Roses," page 45; and the individual entries in the "Encyclopedia of Flowering Vines," pages 52 through 103.)

Protection: Gardeners in cold regions should protect their marginally hardy vines by mulching their bases. Both soil (bring it in—don't dig around the vine) and organic matter, such as compost, are effective; apply the mulch once the ground begins to freeze. To provide even more protection, wrap the vine's topgrowth with burlap. In hot areas, it may be necessary to provide vines with afternoon shade. A few vines are tolerant of salt air—bougainvillea is one—but most are not. Barriers are rarely successful, so coastal gardeners are better off planting climbers that will succeed in oceanside settings.

VINES IN CONTAINERS

Containers not only allow those without garden space a chance to enjoy the beauty of vines, they permit gardeners in cold regions to cultivate frost-tender species.

If your vine will live in a container, be sure to choose a home that is large and sturdy enough, especially if you're growing a perennial species. Pot, tub, barrel, or box; clay, ceramic, plastic, wood, or metal—any container will do as long as it has good drainage. A commercial potting mix to which compost and vermiculite (or perlite) has been added is a good growing medium for container vines. Install a support at the same time you plant in the container. If the support is anchored in the soil, be sure the container is heavy enough that it won't capsize when the vine climbs.

Container-grown vines should be watched carefully, as they can become dehydrated quickly on hot, sunny days. Keep the soil moist but not soggy. Container-grown vines also need to be fed regularly; use a liquid organic fertilizer applied at half strength. Finally, vines grown in containers require regular pruning and should be repotted every three or four years.

Following are species that adapt well to life in pots and tubs.

Balloon vine (*Cardiospermum halicacabum*)
Black-eyed Susan vine (*Thunbergia alata*)
Bougainvilleas (*Bougainvillea* cultivars)
Carolina jessamine (*Gelsemium sempervirens*)
Confederate or star jasmine (*Trachelospermum jasminoides*)
Coral vine (*Antigonon leptopus*)
Cup and saucer vine (*Cobaea scandens*)
Golden-trumpet vine (*Allamanda cathartica*)
Hyacinth bean (*Lablab purpureus*)
Jasmines (*Jasminum* species)
Mandevillas (*Mandevilla* species)
Moonflower (*Ipomoea alba*)
Morning glories (*Ipomoea* species)
Nasturtium (*Tropaeolum majus*)
Passionflowers (*Passiflora* species)
Scarlet runner bean (*Phaseolus coccineus*)

Nasturtiums are happy in containers; the flowers, leaves, and seed pods are edible.

CHAPTER FOUR

CLEMATIS: THE QUEEN OF VINES

by Richard Hawke

JUST THE MENTION OF CLEMATIS evokes a range of responses from gardeners. Some exclaim the wonder of a large-flowered clematis, while others quickly declare their favorite cultivar or two (or three!). Another questions how best to prune his clematis, and still someone else laments the loss of a prized plant to wilt. Whatever the initial responses, the consensus seems to be that everyone loves clematis for its beauty, glorious forms, and profusion of color.

An extraordinary diversity of flower colors, sizes, and forms occurs in the genus *Clematis*. Colors range from shades and blends of blue and red to yellow and white. Flowers can measure from less than one inch across to over six inches wide, and are shaped like urns, bells, stars, and flutes. An interesting floral trait of clematis is the presence of colorful, showy sepals and inconspicuous or absent petals. Sepals—or tepals, as they are sometimes called—vary from four to eight per clematis flower. Seed heads are also ornamental; in many species, they resemble feathery, sil-

Clematis flowers grow in an astonishing array of sizes, shapes, and colors.

Choose a clematis according to your climate and when you'd like to see flowers. For example, 'Perle d'Azur' does well in cold regions and blooms in late summer.

ver puffballs that cover a plant later in the season and account for the common name "old man's beard."

WHO'S WHO

It is common in garden books and nursery catalogs to use the bloom times, flower forms, and pruning requirements of clematis to divide them into three large groups. These groups are not scientific or taxonomic but are instead practical, devised to help gardeners determine where to position a clematis and how to care for it.

Depending upon where you live, the first group of clematis to bloom do so in late winter to early spring on wood produced in the previous season.

The gently nodding flowers of *Clematis alpina* and *C. macropetala* come in purple, blue, pink, and white. Recommended cultivars of *C. alpina* include 'Columbine', 'Frances Rivis', 'Frankie', 'Pamela Jackman', 'Pink Flamingo', and 'Willy'. Noteworthy *C. macropetala* cultivars are 'Blue Bird', 'Jan Lindmark', 'Lagoon', 'Markham's Pink', and 'White Swan'. There are also a number of winter-blooming species suitable for growing in the warmer hardiness zones of the United States (see page 39).

　C. montana and its cultivars also bloom in spring to early summer. They are not reliably hardy in Zone 5, but in warmer areas they produce breathtaking floral displays. Outstanding cultivars include 'Elizabeth', 'Freda', 'Gothenburg', 'Marjorie', 'Odorata', 'Pink Perfection', and 'Wilsonii'.

　The second group of clematis contains the large-flowered cultivars that bloom in early to midsummer, as well as the semidouble and double forms. Flowers are produced on stems that ripen the previous season and, given good care, the plants likely will flower again in late summer. Group 2 contains some of the most popular early, large-flowering cultivars, such as 'Asao', 'Bees Jubilee', 'Carnaby', 'Dr. Ruppel', 'Elsa Spath', 'Fireworks', 'Fujimusume', 'Guernsey Cream', 'Haku Ookan', 'Ken Donson', 'Lasurstern', 'Miss Bateman', 'Mrs. Cholmondeley', 'Mrs. P.B. Truax', 'Nelly Moser', 'Niobe', 'The President', and 'Will Goodwin'.

　The midseason clematis have some of the largest blossoms of all, often six to eight inches across, although not borne in the profusion of the early-flowering cultivars. Recommended plants include 'Crimson King', 'General Sikorski', 'Henryi', 'Marie Boisselot', 'Ramona', and 'Serenata'. The double-flowered cultivars often produce single blossoms on new stems during a second bloom period later in the season. Recommended cultivars include 'Arctic Queen', 'Daniel Deronda', 'Mrs. P.T. James', 'Royalty', and 'Vyvyan Pennell'.

　The third group comprises the late-season clematis and contains a good number of large-flowered cultivars as well as many interesting species and the viticellas. Flowers are produced on the current season's stems; in northern areas, these blooms appear from late June to August and September. Probably the best known large-flowered type is *C. × jackmanii*, a hybrid that dates back more than 100 years and is still popular today. Other notable cultivars include 'Ascotiensis', 'Comtesse de Bouchaud', 'Ernest Markham', 'Hagley Hybrid', 'Huldine', 'John Paul II', 'Lady Betty Balfour', 'Madame Edouard Andre', 'Perle d'Azur', 'Rouge Cardinal', 'Star of India', and 'Ville de Lyon'.

　The late-flowering clematis are many and contain both hardy and ten-

Sometimes called "old man's beard," many clematis have ornamental seed heads.

der species. Many of these species, including *C. orientalis, C. tangutica, C. terniflora, C. texensis,* and *C. vitalba,* are vigorous and produce copious flowers each year. The flowers and subsequent fruit of sweet autumn clematis (*C. terniflora*) or 'Bill Mackenzie' (*C. orientalis*) are striking in their profusion and charm.

The viticellas, too, are a valuable and versatile group of vines. Aside from being prolific bloomers and vigorous growers, viticellas are not troubled by wilt. Flowers come in a variety of colors and are usually smaller than three inches across. The flowers can be nodding and somewhat cup-shaped to almost fully flat. Within this floriferous group are the recommended cultivars 'Betty Corning', 'Etoile Violette', 'Grandiflora Sanguinea' ('Sodertalje'), 'Little Nell', 'Madame Julia Correvon', 'Minuet', 'Polish Spirit', 'Purpurea Plena Elegans', 'Royal Velvet', and 'Venosa Violacea'.

NOTEWORTHY CLEMATIS

OVERLOOKED SPECIES WITH SMALL FLOWERS

Clematis aethusifolia
C. campaniflora
C. connata
C. × *cylindrica*
C. fargesioides
C. fusca
C. akebioides
C. koreana
C. pitcheri
C. potaninii
C. rehderiana
C. tibetana
C. viorna

CLEMATIS FOR WARM REGIONS

Clematis addisonii
C. armandii
C. campaniflora
C. cirrhosa
C. flammula
C. florida
C. montana
C. paniculata
C. rehderiana
C. × *vedrariensis*

CLEMATIS FOR COLD REGIONS

Clematis alpina 'Pamela Jackman'
C. a. 'Ascotiensis'
C. a. 'Bees Jubilee'
C. a. 'Bill Mackenzie'
C. a. 'Comtesse de Bouchaud'
C. a. 'Elsa Späth'
C. a. 'Ernest Markham'
C. a. 'Gipsy Queen'
C. a. 'Guernsey Cream'
C. a. 'Hagley Hybrid'
C. × *jackmanii*
C. × *jackmanii* 'John Paul II'
C. × *jackmanii* 'Lady Betty Balfour'
C. macropetala 'Marie Boisselot'
C. m. 'Mrs. Cholmondeley'
C. m. 'Mrs. P.B. Truax'
C. m. 'Nelly Moser'
C. m. 'Pagoda'
C. m. 'Perle d'Azur'
C. m. 'Rouge Cardinal'
C. tangutica 'The President'
C. t. 'Ville de Lyon'
C. viticella 'Vyvyan Pennell'

CULTURE & TRAINING

A well-grown clematis will give you years of pleasure. Selecting the right clematis *and* the right place in your garden to plant it are hand-in-hand decisions. Like most vines, clematis responds to sunlight with greater plant vigor and increased flower production. But clematis also requires a cool, moist soil for optimum growth. Planting clematis with its base protected by the shade of a shrub or tree, or underplanting with a groundcover, a perennial, or an organic mulch will provide a cool root zone.

Newly planted clematis need liberal amounts of water until established, and then should not be allowed to dry out. Do not plant clematis where it will have to compete for water, such as too close to a large tree trunk, or in the dry area near a wall or building with overhanging eaves. Vines won't tolerate soggy soils either. An organic mulch, such as compost or rotted manure, does double duty by conserving water and shading the roots.

When adding clematis to your garden, make the planting hole at least 12 inches deep and wide. Compost or rotted manure and peat moss can be mixed with the topsoil and placed back into the hole to provide a good growing medium. Experts disagree on whether or not to plant clematis deeply. The theory is that a crown buried two to four inches beneath the soil can assist with regeneration of stems from dormant buds if the top of the plant is damaged by animals, wilt, or mechanical injury. It doesn't hurt to plant a clematis deeply and doing so might be insurance for the future. The thick roots of the large-flowered cultivars should be gently loosened if pot-bound at planting time, but disturbing the fibrous roots of many species can have disastrous results. Handle with care!

The best time to plant clematis—either in spring to early summer or late summer to fall—used to depend upon your climate. However, planting can occur at almost any time of the year now that containerized specimens are commonly available, especially if sufficient water is given after planting. Established clematis can be transplanted in early spring before bud break by cutting the stems back hard to strong buds and digging a root ball two feet in diameter. Large-flowered clematis are easier to transplant than the fibrous-rooted species.

Don't postpone supporting new plants. Securing the stems is an important consideration at planting time. Insert a stake near the crown to begin training the plant upward to its intended position. Care taken during initial training will decrease the need for severe pruning later in the life of the clematis. It is a good practice to prune a clematis hard—to about 12 inches before bud break—the first spring after planting. This encourages

Clematis requires cool, moist soil for optimum growth.

branching, which will establish a strong framework of stems at the base of the plant.

Fertilize clematis in early spring before flower buds start to swell. An organic compost or rotted manure, the ideal fertilizer, also acts as a mulch to retain moisture and cool the root zone. If compost is unavailable, a balanced liquid or granular organic fertilizer can be used before flowering begins.

PRUNING GUIDELINES

Pruning clematis may seem a daunting exercise, even to an experienced gardener. A mystique has grown up around the pruning process, creating a perception of difficulty that is mostly unwarranted. Simpy put, the bloom period determines to which group a clematis belongs and when and how it should be pruned. Familiarity with the clematis you are growing will help you determine the best pruning method. It is easy to oversimplify the procedure and there are always exceptions, but a few guidelines will assist you in making basic pruning decisions.

• **Group 1** includes the earliest-flowering species such as *C. alpina, C. macropetala*, and *C. montana*. Flowers are produced on the previous season's wood, and plants should be pruned after flowering is finished. New stems that develop after pruning will eventually produce the flower buds for the following spring. Pruning is only necessary if space is limited or to remove dead and weak stems. Severe pruning late in the season will reduce the next year's crop of flowers.

• **Group 2** includes the early and midseason large-flowered cultivars. Their first flowers typically open before mid-June on stems arising from the previous season's wood. Prune in late winter or early spring when buds begin to swell but stems have not yet started to grow. Prune out any weak and dead stems, and cut back remaining stems to a pair of strong, healthy buds. How far back you cut the stems will be determined by when you want the plants to bloom. Plants will bloom later if pruned hard early in the season or if killed back in winter. This group will often flower on new wood again in late summer or fall.

• **Group 3** includes the late-blooming, large-flowered cultivars, and the late-flowering species that bloom on new stems each year. Stems usually die during the winter and must be removed before new growth begins in the spring. Stems may live through a mild winter, but plants will become leggy and overgrown if not cut back regularly. Like Group 2, pruning should be completed in late winter or early spring. Prune the old growth to a pair of healthy, strong buds near the base of the plant, or right down to the ground. Hard pruning encourages new shoots from the crown.

Be sure to tie stems into place immediately following pruning. Many clematis grow so quickly in the spring that daily attention to training is necessary, and such care will reward you with a better display. Plastic-coated wire, plastic mesh, or wooden lath can be used to support the clematis on a wall or fence. The natural fiber raffia is a good choice for tying the stems to their supports until the clematis can cling on its own.

DISEASE & PESTS

Clematis are not bothered by many diseases or pests, but wilt can be debilitating. Clematis wilt is most damaging during the early part of the growing season, when the plants are in bud or just beginning to flower. Leaf spot and/or partial stem rot occurs, then the vine wilts and withers because moisture cannot reach the growing tips. This can happen slowly or quickly and can affect just one stem or an entire plant.

All the more frustrating, the experts disagree on whether wilt is a cultural problem or is caused by a fungus. Fungicides have been used as a preventative; however, once the plant has been infected, the only recommended control is to prune out affected stems below the infection point. Experts do seem to agree that clematis wilt is usually not fatal, and most plants will resprout from below the infected point—some even after several years of being presumed dead. Although the causes are unclear, it is important to follow good cultural practices, as healthy plants are less susceptible to wilt.

Earwigs, slugs, rabbits, and mice can also damage clematis. Earwigs cause injury to leaves, flowers, and flower buds, but in most cases the damage is only cosmetic. Treatment against slugs is the same as for any other plants prone to their damage: Pull back any mulch and set out traps. A wire mesh cage placed around the stems of clematis, to at least 24" high, is a good deterrent against rabbits and may also keep mice from nesting at the base of the plant.

With amazingly few demands, clematis will reward you with an abundance of beautiful blossoms. Be creative. Take advantage of the many flower forms and colors by combining more than one plant for interesting effects and a prolonged bloom display.

And remember that there is a clematis for just about any situation—to cover an arbor, to climb a pole or post, to ramble through the garden border or along a wall. Choose wisely, and you will be rewarded with extravagant blossoms for many years. To see a clematis in full bloom is to understand why it is often called the queen of flowering vines.

CHAPTER FIVE

CLIMBING ROSES

by Robert Osborne

IF YOU FOLLOW the strict definition of a vine—a climbing plant—the category would not include roses. Their stems do not twine, nor do they form modified leaf structures such as tendrils or sucker pads, as do true vines. They are, however, one of the most popular plants for training on vertical structures, such as trellises, walls, arbors, fences, and posts. There are a few species that do use their hooked thorns to gain a foothold on shrubs and trees, but most of these are grown only in the mildest climates.

The term "climbing rose," then, is not a botanical classification. It is a classification of convenience for gardeners. Simply put, roses that are called climbers are species and cultivars that produce shoots that are long enough to make them suitable for tying to vertical structures.

It is important to choose species and cultivars that will thrive at your site. Trying to grow a climbing rose that needs protection during winter, for example, creates nearly insurmountable problems in a cold climate. 'John Cabot', 'William Baffin', and 'Henry Kelsey' lead the list of cold-

'William Baffin' is a good choice for cold climates and is also resistant to disease.

tolerant climbing roses.

Climbing roses are variable in their hardiness and resistance to disease and insect damage, so it is important to choose roses that suit your cultural temperament. For instance, if you don't want to use pesticides, it is foolish to grow roses that are prone to disease. 'John Davis', 'Polka', 'New Dawn', and 'William Baffin' are four cultivars with better-than-average disease resistance.

WHERE TO PLANT

Be sure that the site you choose for your climbing rose is well drained. Roses need moisture to thrive, but if water fills the air spaces in the soil, the roots will suffocate from lack of oxygen. If the soil is not well drained, you must provide drainage. Unfortunately, digging a hole and filling the bottom with crushed stone won't solve a drainage problem. You must provide a drain pipe running from below the root zone (usually 18 to 24 inches deep) to an exit point. Your drain pipe should have a slope of at least one-eighth inch per running foot. If you can't provide such drainage, then you must build a raised bed so that the rose roots can grow well above the saturated soil.

Roses also need sun. Full sun. Plants grown in partial shade will be spindly, will produce few flowers, and will be more susceptible to diseases and insects. If your site doesn't get at least six hours of full sun, find another place to grow climbing roses.

Last, gardeners living in colder climates must locate climbing roses so that they are protected in winter from cold north and west winds. Southern and eastern exposures against houses are good sites; large evergreens, walls, and fences can provide protection as well.

FROM THE GROUND UP

The quality of your soil determines the quality of your roses. Soils usually fall between the extremes of pure sand and pure clay. Soil that is balanced between sand and clay provides the ideal conditions for the growth of healthy roses.

As a gardener, your job is to keep the soil balanced, active, and healthy. The secret to improving sandy soil is the addition of organic matter, or humus. Although clay soils also benefit from the addition of organic matter, your approach should be different. Instead of improving the soil in the planting hole, which would abruptly change the continuity of soil texture, plant in the existing clay soil—avoiding deep planting—and add composts and mulches to the surface. The roots will be able to obtain oxygen and nutrients in the soil directly below the mulched surface. If roses are mulched with composts and other organic matter throughout the year, the soil will become more friable and loamy over time.

Another important characteristic of soil is its acidity. Roses grow best in a pH near neutral or just slightly acidic (pH 6.5 to 7.0). If your soil is highly acidic, you can neutralize it by adding ground agricultural limestone. If your soil is too alkaline, add sulfur or sphagnum peat. Many state Extension Service offices and university schools of agriculture provide soil tests; the results will indicate your soil's pH and, if necessary, will recommend how to adjust it to the proper level.

SOMETHING TO EAT

Nitrogen is often called the critical element because plants cannot directly absorb it from the air. By adding blood meal, fish meal, or other high-protein supplements such as soymeal, cottonseed meal, linseed meal, or alfalfa meal to your soil, you can ensure that your roses will get plenty of nitrogen. Another excellent way to provide nitrogen is to add compost to your soil. It improves both the fertility and tilth of soil.

THE ROOT OF THE THING

Most roses are grown by grafting, or budding, a named cultivar on a suitable rootstock. This technique is centuries old and produces vigorous growth. But there are disadvantages to grafting. The rootstock will usually produce suckers, shoots that are not from the plant the gardener wants. These suckers must be pruned off; otherwise, the rootstock suckers will use much of the plant's energy and may outgrow the cultivar growing on top of the rootstock. Additionally, many rootstocks are more tender than the cultivars budded on them, which can cause winter injury.

Before you buy, find out whether your rose is budded or growing on its own roots. Fortunately, own-root roses—roses propagated from cuttings or microcuttings—are becoming increasingly available to home gardeners. However, if your plant is budded, make sure that the rootstock is hardy in your USDA zone. When planting a budded rose, bury the graft union two to four inches below the soil surface. This will help discourage suckering and will encourage the desired variety to produce roots of its own.

PUTTING DOWN ROOTS

Whether by mail or from the local nursery, most roses come either bare-rooted or planted in a container. When you receive a bare-root rose—the usual form if you buy mail-order—be sure to keep the roots moist and shaded until planting. If you cannot plant a rose in its final site within a day or two, give it a temporary home in a corner of your garden or bury its roots in damp sawdust or peat moss until you have time to move it to its permanent home.

Remember, too, that rose roots grow more laterally than vertically, so the width of your planting hole is more important than its depth. Dig a hole that gives plenty of room for horizontal growth and is just deep enough to set the rose at the same depth it was growing before. In light soils, incorporate soil amendments such as compost or well-rotted manure, a small handful of bonemeal, and a small handful of blood meal or fish meal. Add lime in acidic soils. Mix these amendments into the soil that will be placed over the carefully spread roots. In clay soils, plant back into the clay and place composts, rotted manures, and other amendments

Continues on page 50

BEST OF THE CLIMBERS

Hundreds of rose cultivars can be used effectively as climbers. Following are a few of the most treasured.

'Albertine'. A large-flowered, light pink rambler. One showy display in early summer. Fragrant and quite hardy. Zone 5.

'Alchymist'. A very double, modern, apricot flower with an old garden rose form. Vigorous and fragrant. Once-blooming and hardy. Zone 5.

'Blush Noisette'. An old and famous Noisette climber. The clove-scented flowers are produced continuously in clusters. Excellent for warmer regions. Zone 7.

'Constance Spry'. The first of David Austin's English roses. Very vigorous canes. Flowers are immense pink doubles that resemble peonies. Once-blooming but showy. Scented and hardy. Zone 5.

'Dorothy Perkins'. An older rambler that produces small pink blooms in large clusters. Once-blooming. Little scent. Zones 5 to 9.

'Excelsa'. A vigorous, hardy rose, deep pink to red. Zone 5.

'Golden Showers'. A bright yellow, climbing floribunda. Repeat bloom. Light scent. Zone 6.

'Handel'. A climbing floribunda with white petals that flush to pink at the edges. Repeat bloom. Light scent. Zone 6.

'Henry Kelsey'. A modern pillar rose with long shoots that carry clusters of deep red blooms with yellow stamens. Lightly scented and very hardy. Zones 3 to 4.

'Iceberg Climbing'. A showy, white floribunda climber. Repeat flowering but very little scent. Zone 6.

'John Cabot'. Double, light red to deep orchid pink *kordesii* pillar rose that repeats. Disease resistant with light scent. Very hardy. Zones 3 to 4.

'Maigold'. A modern, deep yellow with orange tones. Once-blooming. Good scent. Vigorous and hardy. Zone 5.

'New Dawn'. The most popular climber. Soft, blowsy, pink blooms on a vigorous plant. Lightly scented. Zones 5 to 6.

'Paul's Scarlet Climber'. A continuously blooming, scarlet red climber that's vigorous. No scent. Zone 6.

'William Baffin'. A vigorous and very healthy pillar rose with bright pink, semi-double blooms. Light scent. Perhaps the most hardy climber. Zone 3.

FOR SOUTHERN GARDENS

Among the helpful lists in Lois Trigg Chaplin's *The Southern Gardener's Book of Lists* (1994) is this one, "Roses That Climb and Ramble." All the cultivars are hardy to Zone 6, will reach 12 feet or more, and are repeat bloomers.

'Climbing Cécile Brünner' (light pink)
'Climbing Crimson Glory'
'Climbing Iceberg' (white)
'Climbing Lady Hillingdon' (light apricot-yellow)
'Climbing Perle des Jardins' (yellow)
'Climbing Souvenir de la Malmaison' (pale pink)
'Clytemnestra' (apricot-pink)
'Dortmund' (red)
'Jaune Desprez' (pale apricot)
'Kathleen'
'Lamarque' (yellowish white)
'Madame Alfred Carriére' (pale pink to white)
'Mermaid' (primrose-yellow)
'New Dawn' (pale pearl-pink)
'Skyrocket'

FOR THE PACIFIC NORTHWEST

Ray and Jan McNeilan include climbing roses in their *Pacific Northwest Gardener's Book of Lists* (1997). They advise training climbing roses with "as many horizontal runs as possible, as this is where the most flowers will be grown."

'Royal Sunset' thrives in the Northwest.

'Altissimo' (medium red)
'Dortmund' (medium red)
'Dublin Bay' (medium red)
'Golden Showers' (medium yellow)
'Iceberg' (white)
'Jeanne Lajoie' (light pink)
'Royal Sunset' (apricot blend)
'Zéphirine Drouhin' (medium pink)

For Northwest gardeners west of the Cascades:
'Handel' (red blend)
'Fred Loads' (orange)
'Jeanne Lajoie' (medium pink)
'Joseph's Coat' (red blend)
'Royal Sunset' (apricot blend)

on the surface. After planting, mulch the rose with two or three inches of rotted bark or a similar material.

Follow the same instructions for potted roses, but inspect the root ball carefully before you set it in the hole. If the roots are circling and matted, tease them free, or make several shallow vertical cuts down the root ball with a clean, sharp knife. This will free the roots and allow them to grow outward.

Once your rose is planted, water the area thoroughly. Keep new transplants well watered throughout their first season. Providing adequate moisture is the most important part of establishing new roses—but be careful and avoid over-watering, especially in heavy clay soils. Too much water is as harmful as too little.

THE PATH UP: TRAINING AND PRUNING

Training a climbing rose is an ongoing process. New shoots are the most pliable. When the wood turns from soft to slightly stiff, tie the canes to the structure you have provided. Be sure to use tie materials that will not chafe the stems, and tie canes loosely, so that they will be able to increase their diameter as they mature.

Training and pruning go hand in hand; pruning is a valuable tool to shape your rose, to train it to climb, and to discourage disease and insect infections. Fortunately, roses have a remarkable ability to thrive despite our efforts to shape them to our desires.

Pruning should be guided by a sense of purpose. Begin by removing any dead or diseased wood. Next, decide which canes will form the main framework of the plant. Remove any canes that compete for light with the chosen canes. Stepping back from your work to look at the entire plant will help to guide your choices.

As a general rule, prune young roses lightly to encourage a strong root system. As the more vigorous shoots appear, begin to form the vertical structure. As these shoots mature, prune out a few of them each year to encourage new shoots. A small amount of careful pruning each year will result in a healthier climbing rose than a heavy pruning every few years will. And a far better-looking one.

The structures you use to support your climbing rose are limited only by your imagination. Roses are most commonly grown on trellises, pergolas, and arches. They are also trained to grow horizontally along fences—rambling species are particularly effective for this purpose—and even up poles, forming what might pass for living pillars. Walls are effective backdrops for climbing roses, although they will need hooks or wires where the canes can be tied.

Training and pruning of climbing roses, like this 'Noisette Carnée', go hand-in-hand.

ENCYCLOPEDIA

OF

FLOWERING VINES

by Lewis Hill, Nancy Hill, and Peter Loewer

Actinidia polygama

SILVER VINE

A hardy, deciduous perennial, silver vine twines as it climbs, producing a heavy mass of large, heart-shaped, faintly variegated leaves. Clusters of fragrant 1" white flowers, which appear in early summer, are a bonus. Male and female blossoms are on separate plants, so you will need one of each to produce the small yellow edible fruits. The vine is resistant to insects and disease but attractive to cats, who delight in destroying young plants.

NATIVE HABITAT: Eastern Asia

USDA HARDINESS ZONE: 4

HABIT & GARDEN USE: Growing to 30', silver vine will create a dense screen for a sunny terrace or a private area in the yard. Be patient, for it takes some time for a new vine to start growing well.

HOW TO GROW: Silver vines do best in fertile, organically rich soil and strong light—either full sun or light shade. Mature vines should be cut back in late winter to encourage heavier blooms the following year.

CULTIVARS & RELATED SPECIES: The hardy kiwi or tara vine (*A. arguta*, Zone 4) bears smaller fruits than the fuzzy type sold in supermarkets. It is a twining vine, and both foliage and fruit are edible. The famil-

Silver vine (above) and related kiwi vine are good for creating dense screens.

iar supermarket kiwi fruit *A. deliciosa* (Zone 7) has tropical-looking foliage, grows to 25', and bears white flowers that turn to orange-yellow. The 12' *A. kolomikta* (Zone 4) has variegated foliage of pink, red, and deep green, and small white fragrant flowers. 'Arctic', which has pink, white, and green leaves, is unusually hardy.

Akebia quinata

AKEBIA
Five-leaf akebia, chocolate vine

A vigorous semi-evergreen grower—to 40'—akebia sometimes becomes weedy but is easily controlled by pruning. The compound, vividly green leaves are five-segmented, suggesting the scientific name, and the autumn and winter leaves' rich brown alludes to the common name. Clusters of small, fragrant, purple male

and female flowers appear in spring; the sausagelike purple fruits, which are infrequent, are edible.

NATIVE HABITAT: Korea, Japan, and China

USDA HARDINESS ZONE: 5

HABIT & GARDEN USE: Akebia is an attractive perennial twiner to use on trellises, arbors, or pergolas, to cover

Five-leaf akebia

a steep bank, or to trail along a fence. The leaves stay green in the South during the winter, but they darken and hang on in colder regions.

HOW TO GROW: Akebia is easy to grow in ordinary, even poor, soil and withstands either sun or moderate shade. Plants need little care and are so energetic that you can cut them to the ground in the fall and they will grow back the next summer.

CULTIVARS & RELATED SPECIES: *A. trifoliata* (Zone 5), which has three-segmented leaves, is deciduous and considered less attractive than *A. quinata.*

Allamanda cathartica

GOLDEN-TRUMPET VINE
Common allamanda

Easily grown, this robust quasi-twining—it leans more than it twines—vine is a member of the milkweed fam-

Golden-trumpet vine

ily. A shrubby tender perennial, it reaches 25' in the wild and has whorls of glossy evergreen leaves; the fragrant 4" golden-yellow, funnel-shaped flowers first appear in spring, but plants bloom for 6 months and longer in warm regions. Plants are poisonous.

NATIVE HABITAT: South American tropics

USDA HARDINESS ZONE: 10

HABIT & GARDEN USE: One of the best and most carefree flowering vines for warm conditions, allamandas also do well in pots—clay, not plastic—in cold regions and indoors as greenhouse or houseplants. They are superb for terrace plantings and training along garden walls and fences, and can climb poles or tripods if their stems are tied to the support.

HOW TO GROW: Indoors, allamandas need at least 5 hours of sun. Outdoors, they like full sun or light shade and organically rich, well-drained soil. For potted plants, use a sterile mix composed of 1 part potting soil, 1 part composted cow manure, and 1 part sharp sand. Container plants require moist soil and perfect drainage—water daily and apply a balanced organic fertilizer at ½ strength every 2 or 3 weeks. After growth ceases in the fall, water sparingly and allow the vine to rest. In cold regions, overwinter indoors in a cool, bright location. Prune in spring to control growth.

CULTIVARS & RELATED SPECIES: 'Compacta' is a small cultivar, easily kept under 2'; 'Grandiflora' is free-flowering with large blossoms; the yellow flowers of 'Hendersonii' are tinged with bronze; 'Williamsii' bears large double flowers. Purple allamanda (*A. blanchetti*) has bell-shaped purple flowers and is usually grafted onto *A. cathartica* rootstock.

Ampelopsis arborea

PEPPER VINE

Pepper vine

Pepper vine , a too-rarely-cultivated native vine, is a woody perennial with lustrous toothed leaves that turn red in autumn. It grows to 15' and produces clusters of small greenish flowers followed by fruits that begin their careers colored white, then turn currant-red, and wind up glossy blue-black.

NATIVE HABITAT: Southeastern U.S.

USDA HARDINESS ZONE: 7

HABIT & GARDEN USE: Pepper vine is fine for covering walls, arbors, and fences. It has a bushy habit and makes a fine screen or groundcover.

HOW TO GROW: Moist but well-drained, fertile soil is preferable for this woodland climber. Fruiting will be heaviest in a sunny site.

CULTIVARS & RELATED SPECIES: Monk's-hood vine (*A. aconitifolia*, Zone 4), has greenish white blooms followed by brown-orange berries. The most commonly cultivated ampelopsis, *A. brevipedunculata*, has become an invasive weed along the Northeast coast.

Antigonon leptopus

CORAL VINE
Love's chain, queen's wreath, Mexican creeper, Confederate vine, mountain rose

Bright green, textured arrow- and heart-shaped leaves to 4" act as perfect foils for the long racemes, or clusters, of small rose-pink flowers. The blooms, which appear from midsummer through fall, have darker pink centers. A tender perennial, coral vine is evergreen in the warmest parts of its range and deciduous elsewhere. The vine's tubers are edible.

NATIVE HABITAT: Mexico

USDA HARDINESS ZONES: 8 to 9

HABIT & GARDEN USE: Coral vine has tendrils that help it reach 30', but new plants need to be tied to begin the climb. Vines killed back by cold temperatures will recover quickly. Fast growing, coral vine is ideal for

Moths hover over cruel vine's waxy, pale blossoms on summer nights.

screening on porches and balconies, for covering fences, arbors, and pergolas, and is a fine candidate for growing up a tree. It also does well in pots and is an excellent cut flower. In cold regions, cultivate coral vine in a container and overwinter indoors.

HOW TO GROW: Coral vines need full sun, modestly fertile sandy or light soil that drains well, moderate moisture when they are actively growing, and less water when they are resting. They are highly sensitive to cold; vines in marginally warm regions should be mulched. In ideal conditions, plants may bloom almost continuously. Flowers are produced on new wood, so prune in late winter, if necessary.

CULTIVARS & RELATED SPECIES: 'Album' has white flowers; 'Baja Red' is hot pink.

Araujia sericifera

CRUEL VINE
Cruel plant, bladder vine

Cruel vine is an intensely fragrant plant with white or pale pink, waxy, bell-shaped blossoms, $\frac{1}{2}$" wide, that appear in summer and fall. The flowers, the inside of which may be slightly striped with purple, are attractive to moths on warm summer nights. Insects stick to the pollen, hence the common name "cruel vine." A perennial member of the milkweed family, cruel vine climbs by twining.

NATIVE HABITAT: Southern Brazil
USDA HARDINESS ZONES: 8 to 9
HABIT & GARDEN USE: Unless you garden in a frost-free area, cultivate

this fast-growing climber—up to 30'—in a container backed by a strong trellis. Overwinter container plants in a bright, cool location. In warmer regions, cruel vine is superb when planted against a garden wall or fence. Large, pear-shaped fruit pods produce a mass of seeds, each with a tuft of silky threads.

HOW TO GROW: Few nurseries sell cruel vine, so start from seeds; germination takes 3 to 6 weeks, with seedlings usually blooming about 10 months later. Plants prefer a moderately moist soil and a spot in filtered sun or light shade. Pruning is usually not needed, but if vines become leggy, cut them back; the stem's white sap will form a crust that prevents further bleeding.

CULTIVARS & RELATED SPECIES: None widely available.

Aristolochia macrophylla

DUTCHMAN'S PIPE
Pipe vine

This woody-stemmed, twining perennial was an especially popular plant at the turn of the century, when it made an ideal drape for that era's large Victorian houses. Large (6" to 10"), glossy, dark green, heart-shaped, overlapping leaves make this deciduous climber perfect for screening or for shading terraces and decks. The plant's common name comes from the small, inconspicuous, purple-brown flowers, which appear in summer and are shaped like meerschaum pipes. The flowers have an unusual but not offensive odor.

NATIVE HABITAT: North America
USDA HARDINESS ZONE: 4
HABIT & GARDEN USE: Its rank growth—30' and higher—makes Dutchman's pipe unsuitable for most small gardens. You'll need a strong trellis, wall, or pergola to support its weight, and when grown on a building, Dutchman's pipe can hold moisture so efficiently that over time it may rot wood shingles.

HOW TO GROW: Dutchman's pipe grows well in sun or partial shade, withstands urban pollution, and thrives in ordinary, well-drained soil. Plants need plenty of moisture during the growing season and often take a couple of years before they grow rapidly. Once established, vines shoot up at lightning speed and are rarely bothered by insects or disease. Prune heavily to keep vines within bounds. To encourage side branching, pinch the ends of the growing shoots frequently during the summer.

CULTIVARS & RELATED SPECIES: Virginia snakeroot (*A. serpentaria*, Zone 8) is a southeastern U.S. native that is sometimes used medicinally. The small flowers of California Dutchman's pipe (*A. californica*, Zone 8) precede the vine's deciduous, heart-shaped leaves. The tropical calico flower (*A. littoralis*, Zone 10) has triangle-shaped, evergreen leaves and 3" purple-veined, white flowers. Pelican, or swan, flower (*A. grandiflora*, Zone 10), which grows to 10', is another tender species for frost-free regions.

Asarina antirrhinifolia

TWINING SNAPDRAGON
Climbing snapdragon, chicabiddy, maurandya, hummingbird vine

A tender perennial vine, twining snapdragon—asarina is Spanish for snapdragon—is widely grown as an annual in cold regions. It reaches a height of 8' when grown as an annual, but is much taller in frost-free regions, where it is perennial. Its leaves are arrow-shaped. In early summer, the vines bear small, trumpet-shaped flowers that are lavender and purple with white throats. There is also a strain that produces red and yellow flowers.

NATIVE HABITAT: Mexico and the Southwest U.S.

USDA HARDINESS ZONE: 9

HABIT & GARDEN USE: Twining snapdragons make excellent container plants and can be overwintered indoors. Outside, they are easily trained to climb strings or a lattice; they can also trail from window boxes or hanging baskets. Twining snapdragons are a fine choice for gardeners with limited space.

HOW TO GROW: Plants are rarely

Twining snapdragons, such as this 'Mystic Pink', make great container plants.

available, so start seeds 8 to 12 weeks before the last frost and plant out when all danger of frost is past; in warm climates, seeds can be sown outdoors. Twining snapdragon prefers full sun and moist, neutral soil that drains well. Remove spent blooms and seed pods to prolong flowering into autumn. When grown as an annual, vines rarely need pruning; pinch back stem tips to promote bushiness.

CULTIVARS & RELATED SPECIES: There are more than a dozen species available. *A. barclaiana* grows to 10' when treated as an annual and has white, pink, and purple blooms. Creeping gloxinia (*A. erubescens*) has 2" rose-pink flowers. *A. scandens* 'Violet Glow' has indigo-blue blooms.

Bignonia capreolata

CROSS-VINE
Quartervine, trumpet flower

Cross-vine

Woody stems, evergreen or semi-evergreen leaves, and showy flowers make fast-growing, under-used cross-vine a great choice for home landscapes (its common name comes from the cross pattern in the stem's pith). Cross-vine climbs by using its twining tendrils that have adhesive disks at their tips. When well grown, cross-vine can reach a height of 50'. Clusters of 2" trumpet-shaped flowers, red-orange outside, yellow and red inside, appear on new wood in late spring, followed by 6" beanlike pods in summer. The vine's compound ovate leaves turn a modest purple-red in the fall, providing winter color.

NATIVE HABITAT: Southeast U.S.
USDA HARDINESS ZONE: 6
HABIT & GARDEN USE: Cross-vine covers most structures with relative ease. An excellent choice for a screen, it prefers a wire fence to a

wall, and is a good vine for a tepee made from wooden stakes or bamboo. It is also a good selection for pergolas, posts, and pillars. Vigorous in warm climates, cross-vine also can be used as a groundcover.

HOW TO GROW: Although able to withstand almost anything, including heat, coastal conditions, thin soil, partial shade, wind, and modest drought, cross-vine can't survive long periods of below-freezing weather. Grow plants in full sun and organically rich, well-drained soil and give them plenty of water for superior flowering. In cold regions, cross-vine can be grown in a container and maintained indoors during winter. It is undemanding in general, and rarely needs pruning.

Propagate from layering, stem cuttings, and seeds. Plants also spread by underground runners.

CULTIVARS & RELATED SPECIES: 'Atrosanguinea', which has narrower leaves than the species, bears dark purple-brown flowers.

Bougainvillea species

BOUGAINVILLEA
Paper flower

Bougainvilleas are popular, shrubby, tropical vines that use their curved thorns and quasi-twining stems to climb. Although its dark green, evergreen foliage is attractive, the bougainvillea's glory is its sweet-pealike flower. As with the poinsettia, the showy portion is actually the three large, papery bracts that surround the true flower, a small, tubular bloom that is usually white or yellow. The bract colors—white, apricot, salmon, pink, red, purple, and orange—are nothing short of dazzling. When grown outdoors, plants have an extremely long bloom time—9 months and more. Mature, healthy plants, which can grow to 30' and are tolerant of salt air, create a solid wall of color.

NATIVE HABITAT: South America
USDA HARDINESS ZONES: 9 to 10
HABIT & GARDEN USE: Whether in the garden or the house, bougainvilleas are the ultimate representatives of tropical living, unsurpassed as canopies for patios, decks, and other outdoor spaces. They are fine plants for screening, for covering walls, arbors, and pergolas, and their cascading habit also makes them superb groundcovers, bank covers, and barriers. Despite their vigor, they are excellent candidates for container culture.

HOW TO GROW: Outdoors, bougainvilleas need full sun for good bloom (in extremely hot conditions, give them midday shade) and moderately fertile, organically rich soil that retains moisture well but is never soggy. Young plants require regular watering, but mature bougainvilleas are drought tolerant. Mature plants also are heavy and require a strong support; young plants must be tied to climb. Prune in late winter or early

Bougainvillea's cascading habit makes it a superb vine for arches or pergolas.

spring to keep plants in bounds or just to shape. In poor soil, feed plants in spring and summer.

Container-grown vines must be pruned regularly to remain manageable. Minimum temperatures should be in the low 50s. Use a medium-large container filled with organically rich soil that drains well; allow the soil to dry out between waterings, especially during the winter months. Feed monthly during spring and summer with a balanced organic fertilizer applied at $1/2$ strength.

Bougainvilleas resent transplanting, so disturb plant roots as little as possible. Experts recommend cutting away the bottom of the pot or can of a container-grown plant. Remove the bottom; next, slit the container from top to bottom. Make a similar cut on the opposite side. Set the plant in a prepared hole, press soil around the container, and then pull out the two halves of the container.

CULTIVARS & RELATED SPECIES: There are scores of named bougainvilleas, either hybrids (such as *B.* × *buttiana*) or cultivars of *B. glabra* or *B. spectabilis*. Among the best are 'Alba' (white), 'Afterglow' (yellow-orange), 'Barbara Karst' (red), 'California Gold' (pale yellow), 'Cherry Blossom' (rose-pink with white centers, double), 'Crimson Jewel' (good container cultivar), 'Don Mario' (purple-red), 'Mary Palmer' (bicolor white and pink), 'Pink Tiara', 'Raspberry Ice' and 'Hawaii' (red, variegated foliage), 'Sanderiana' (purple), 'San Diego Red', 'Tahitian Dawn' (gold aging to rose-purple), 'Texas Dawn' (pink), 'White Madonna', and 'Isabel Greensmith' (orange-red). If you can plant only one bougainvillea, 'San Diego Red', which is also sold as 'Scarlett O'Hara', is a wise choice.

Campsis radicans

TRUMPET CREEPER
Trumpet vine, trumpet flower, cow-itch

A vigorous deciduous vine that holds tightly to stone, brick, or wood with its small aerial rootlets, or holdfasts, trumpet creeper is a colorful plant best suited to large gardens. It grows to 40', developing a trunk-sized main stem over time. Vines produce clusters of 2" or 3" orange-red, funnel-shaped flowers—loved by hummingbirds—beginning in midsummer and lasting well into autumn. The attractive leaves are compound, made up of toothed oval leaflets somewhat reminiscent of the silk tree's. Seed pods, 5" long, appear in fall.

NATIVE HABITAT: Eastern North America

USDA HARDINESS ZONES: 4 to 5

HABIT & GARDEN USE: Useful for shading porches and covering large, rough walls, to which it clings, trumpet creeper is a striking vine when in bloom and also makes a colorful

Hummingbirds love trumpet creeper, whose bold color stands out in large gardens.

groundcover on steep banks. It can also be grown up tall trees. Choose a location the vine won't outgrow quickly—plants can cover one-story buildings without breathing heavily. New plants may need to be tied up until their aerial rootlets develop; older vines, because of their weight, also need sturdy support.

HOW TO GROW: Trumpet creepers are tolerant of wind, poor soil, and partial shade, but full sun is necessary for a generous supply of flowers. Plants prefer organically rich soil that drains well and plenty of moisture (mulch to retain moisture). In many regions, trumpet creepers must be cut back regularly and mowed around to discourage the sprouting seeds and underground runners. To keep plants under control and promote flowering, prune heavily in late winter or early spring. When grown on a building—which isn't recommended, as the rootlets will permanently scar its surface—it may be necessary to cut back or pin upper stems to keep the vine from becoming top-heavy. A sharp spray of water should control aphids, which are occasionally a problem.

CULTIVARS & RELATED SPECIES: 'Flava' (Zone 5), has yellow blooms, 'Crimson Trumpet' (Zone 5) sports red flowers, and 'Madame Galen' (*C. × tagliabuana*) has apricot blossoms (Zone 4). Chinese trumpet vine (*C. grandiflora*) is less vigorous than trumpet creeper, growing to 20', and hardy only to Zone 7; it bears large, 3" scarlet flowers.

Cardiospermum halicacabum

BALLOON VINE
Love-in-a-puff, heart-pea

A tender perennial, balloon vine is most often grown as an annual. It is evergreen in frost-free regions and climbs by tendrils. This attractive plant with square stems and deeply cut, 4" tomatolike leaves bears very small white flowers—which resemble orchids if examined under a lens—in summer. The three-sided light green seed pods that follow, each $1\frac{1}{2}$ inches across, look like bubbles or small balloons against the dark foliage.

Light enough to bounce in the wind, they are so strong you will have to squeeze hard with your fingers to break them. Each seed is marked with a stylized heart shape.

NATIVE HABITAT: Tropical America, India, and Africa

USDA HARDINESS ZONE: 9

HABIT & GARDEN USE: A rambling climber that grows up to 10' in its first season, fast-growing balloon vine needs the support of a trellis, strings, netting, or wire. Although it has tendrils, it may need tying to climb securely. Use for light screening, to cover a wire fence, or simply for the delight its ornamental pods will provide.

HOW TO GROW: Gardeners in cold

Balloon vine is named for its light but amazingly strong, three-sided seed pods.

Birds love American bittersweet's abundant, long-lasting fruits.

regions should sow seeds indoors 3 weeks before the frost-free date; transplant outside when the soil has warmed and the danger of frost has passed. In warmer locations, sow balloon vine seeds directly outdoors. Plants do best in full sun (light shade in extremely hot regions) and organically rich, fertile soil.

CULTIVARS & RELATED SPECIES: Heart-seed (*C. grandiflorum*, Zone 9) has slightly larger leaves and flowers. It is not widely available.

Celastrus scandens

AMERICAN BITTERSWEET

It is the abundant, long-lasting fruits—orange-yellow capsules that split open to reveal red-coated seeds—that are the main attraction of bittersweet. Birds are also fond of the fruits and freely scatter their seeds. Bittersweet is a deciduous, extremely hardy, fast-growing twiner. Small clusters of greenish white flowers, which appear in early summer on new growth, are inconspicuous; however, the toothed, 5" oval leaves turn a pretty yellow in autumn. Vines are rampant, climbing 20' and higher.

NATIVE HABITAT: Eastern North America.

USDA HARDINESS ZONE: 2

HABIT & GARDEN USE: Bittersweet is dioecious—sexes are on different plants—so although both male and female plants flower, both sexes are necessary to produce fruits (on the female plant). One male plant can furnish pollen for many female plants. This vine can become weedy and is best used in a natural or semi-wild situation, such as on a large fence, wall, or pergola where control is not important, or as a groundcover or bank cover.

HOW TO GROW: An unparticular plant, American bittersweet grows well in ordinary soil and in either sun or light shade. These vines need little care and are tolerant of wind and cold—almost anything except wet feet. Other than making sure you have both a male and female plant, you need only provide the vines with a strong support if you want them to climb. To keep growth under control and encourage fruiting, prune heavily in late winter or early spring.

CULTIVARS & RELATED SPECIES: Oriental bittersweet, or staff vine (*C. orbiculatus*, Zones 4 to 5), with dense oval leaves and yellow and pinkish red berries in small, lateral clusters,

has become an invasive weed throughout the East and Midwest. Chinese bittersweet (*C. loeseneri*, Zone 6) grows to 20'. These Asian species, especially Oriental bittersweet, are extremely invasive and should not be planted by gardeners.

Clematis species

CLEMATIS

See "Clematis: The Queen of Vines," page 34.

Cobaea scandens

CUP AND SAUCER VINE
Mexican ivy, monastery bells, cathedral bells, choral bells, violet ivy

A shrubby species, cup and saucer vine climbs by using its foot-long tendrils, which terminate in small, sharp hooks. This climber's 2"-wide, cuplike flowers, which have a modest honey fragrance, begin pale green and eventually turn purple, with faint white striping. Each flower sits on a green saucer-shaped calyx—a collective term for the sepals, outer flower parts that protect the bud—hence the common name. The unusual flowers, which hang upside-down on the vine and appear from midsummer through fall, never fail to delight both children and adults.

NATIVE HABITAT: Mexico and tropical South America

USDA HARDINESS ZONE: 9

HABIT & GARDEN USE: This popular vine can grow as much as 25' in one season. It climbs easily on netting, trellises, arches, pillars, and arbors—in other words, anything it can grasp with its curling tendrils. Cup and saucer vine can also climb on rough-surfaced walls, such as stucco, which it can ascend without help. Compound purple-veined leaves and rapid growth make cup and saucer vine ideal for providing a screen or summer shade. Perennial in warm climates, cup and saucer vine can be grown as an annual in colder regions. Container plants can be overwintered in a greenhouse.

HOW TO GROW: Sow seeds—file them first to speed germination—outdoors in moist, organically rich soil that drains well. In colder regions, sow seeds of cup and saucer vine indoors, 6 to 8 weeks before the last frost. Plants prefer full sun, but afternoon shade is preferable in very hot regions. Don't pour on the fertilizer—overly rich soil will produce leaves at the expense of the cup and saucer vine's unique flowers. Pinch back stem tips to encourage branching and flowering. Prune, if necessary, in early spring.

CULTIVARS & RELATED SPECIES: There is a white-flowered form of cup and saucer vine called 'Alba'.

Glory flower

Eccremocarpus scaber

GLORY FLOWER
Chilean glory flower, glory vine

A tender perennial, glory flower uses its twining tendrils, which terminate in small hooks, to climb. This vine sports clusters of 1"-long, bright orange-red tubular flowers—accurately described by many as looking like goldfish with their mouths open—from summer until the first frost. The twice-compound, bright green oval leaves can have either smooth or toothed margins. Widely cultivated as an annual in cold regions, its ribbed stems become woody in frost-free areas. Long-lasting in the vase, the flowers are popular in the florist trade.

NATIVE HABITAT: Peru and Chile
USDA HARDINESS ZONE: 9
HABIT & GARDEN USE: Frequently grown as a greenhouse plant, glory flower quickly grows to 10' or 12' when treated as an annual. Although it needs something to climb, it does well on all sorts of supports: trellises, strings, wires, walls, and columns. The delicate foliage provides light screening, and since plants expand horizontally as well as vertically, it is a good vine for trailing along fences and covering low supports. Glory flower is often combined with other climbers, such as roses, to provide color in the second half of the gardening season.

HOW TO GROW: Although tolerant of partial shade, glory flower vines should be located in full sun for profuse flowering and sheltered from drying winds. Plants need plenty of water and well-drained, organically rich soil; mulch to retain moisture and to protect roots during the winter in marginal hardiness zones. Sow seeds direct in frost-free gardens; in colder locations, sow seeds in individual containers indoors, then plant out after the danger of frost has passed. Plants usually flower in their first summer. Pinch back stems to promote bushiness; prune in early spring if necessary.

CULTIVARS & RELATED SPECIES: 'Anglia Hybrids Mixed' produces red, yellow, orange, and bicolored flowers; 'Aureus' has yellow flowers; 'Carmineus' blooms in carmine-red; and 'Roseus' bears pink blossoms.

Echinocystis lobata

WILD CUCUMBER
Mock cucumber, prickly cucumber, wild balsam apple, balsam apple

Wild cucumber vines climb to 30' and produce masses of small but lovely, slightly fragrant white flowers beginning in summer and continuing until the first frost. It is perennial in regions with long, hot summers and frost-free winters, and self-sowing in colder climates. Wild cucumber uses tendrils to climb. It is monoecious, so both male and female blooms are produced on the same plant. The male flowers, more ornamental than the female, are those held above the vine on short stems, looking like small bottle brushes. Foliage is lobed, similar to the cucumber's; fruits resemble spiny cucumbers, hence many of the species' common names.

NATIVE HABITAT: North America
USDA HARDINESS ZONE: 8
HABIT & GARDEN USE: While wild cucumber is a first-rate vine for covering arbors, pergolas, and fences, it is even better as a rambler, traveling horizontally along fences, walls, and other low structures. Fast-growing—even weedy in ideal conditions—wild

The fruit of the rambling wild cucumber vine looks like a spiny cucumber.

cucumber can smother a rail fence in a single season.

HOW TO GROW: Wild cucumber does best in a sunny location and in moist soil that is rich in organic matter. Once plants are established, they take care of themselves. Sow seed directly outdoors in warm regions; begin seeds indoors in individual containers in colder areas, transplanting outdoors once the danger of frost has passed. Pruning is unnecessary.

CULTIVARS & RELATED SPECIES: None widely available.

Gelsemium sempervirens

CAROLINA JESSAMINE
Carolina jasmine, yellow jessamine, false jasmine, Carolina wild woodvine, evening trumpet flower

Carolina jessamine is a twining, wiry-stemmed perennial vine in frost-free regions; it will persist as far as Zone 6 if given winter protection. Pairs of narrow, glossy green leaves create a handsome background for Carolina jessamine's bright yellow, 1" trumpet-

Carolina jessamine

like flowers. The blossoms, which open in early spring, are sweetly fragrant, particularly in the evening. All parts of the plant are toxic.

NATIVE HABITAT: Southern U.S., Mexico, and Guatemala

USDA HARDINESS ZONE: 8

HABIT & GARDEN USE: Carolina jessamine is an excellent groundcover, but with a little help will clamber its way up tepee poles and fence posts, even tree trunks and telephone poles. When grown in full sun, the foliage becomes more dense, tight enough to create shade or screening if grown on an arbor or trellis. Although vines grow 20' and taller, Carolina jessamine is a traditional mailbox plant in the South. Plants flower when

young, making them a good choice for container culture, especially hanging baskets.

HOW TO GROW: Carolina jessamine likes its head in the sun, its feet in the shade. Locate plants in full sun in the North, or sun or partial shade in the South. Provide organically rich, well-drained soil, and mulch semiannually with compost. Vines are tolerant of moderate winds and drought but need moisture during the growing season for good flowering. Although vines twine naturally, they may require tying to get started upward. Prune vines immediately after flowering. Container plants can be overwintered indoors: Provide bright indirect light and allow the soil to dry between waterings.

CULTIVARS & RELATED SPECIES: 'Pride of Augusta', also listed as 'Floraplena' and 'Plena', has double flowers but is not an improvement on the species.

Gloriosa superba

GLORY LILY
Gloriosa lily, climbing lily, creeping lily, flame lily

Glory lily is a tender vine grown for its abundance of exotic lilylike blooms, which appear in summer and change color as they mature. Each flower, held singly on a long stalk, consists of six 3"-long, bright red upswept tepals that are yellow at their

base and up their wavy margins, or edges, and long, dramatic stamens. The 5" leaves are lance-shaped and glossy. Glory lily is a tuberous perennial herb that climbs by using tendrils. All parts of the plant are toxic.
NATIVE HABITAT: Tropical Africa and Asia
USDA HARDINESS ZONES: 8 to 9
HABIT & GARDEN USE: An airy vine—each tuber produces only three or four stems that grow to about 6'—glory lily uses the tendrils on the end of its leaves to climb trellises or other supports, such as shrubs or small trees. Tie the stems or allow the plant to sprawl. Stems break easily, so locate glory lily in a protected site. It is an excellent container plant for decks and terraces.
HOW TO GROW: Easy to cultivate where there is a long garden season, glory lilies should be planted in fertile, humus-rich soil in February for summer bloom. The purple "eyes" are easily broken, so be careful when handling the tubers. Choose a sunny location outdoors, with filtered sun in hot regions. Plants need plenty of water during the growing season but never allow the soil to become soggy. In Zone 7 and colder, where glory lily is begun indoors, dig the tubers before the first frost and store them in peat or vermiculite at 40° to 50°F.
CULTIVARS & RELATED SPECIES: There are many named cultivars, including: 'Abyssinica' (red banded with gold), 'Carsonii' (purple-red edged in yellow), 'Citrina' (yellow striped with claret), 'Grandiflora' (golden yellow), and 'Superba' (yellow turning orange-red). 'Rothschildiana', ruby with a yellow base and stripe, is considered the best choice.

Hydrangea petiolaris

CLIMBING HYDRANGEA

Lacy 8" flat clusters of small white fertile flowers encircled by larger sterile blooms and glossy, dark green, 3"-long heart-shaped leaves with fine-toothed margins make this clinging vine a garden favorite. In autumn, its woody stems turn brownish red, its leaves a pretty yellow. Climbing hydrangea, which blooms in summer, is one of the few vines with showy

Climbing hydrangea

flowers that can both cling to surfaces without support and thrive in partial sun. Like ivy, climbing hydrangea uses aerial rootlets to attach itself to vertical surfaces.

NATIVE HABITAT: Japan, Korea, and China

USDA HARDINESS ZONE: 3

HABIT & GARDEN USE: Able to scale huge brick, stone, stucco, or shingled buildings and walls, climbing hydrangea grows up to 65' on any rough surface. It is also an excellent vine for covering tall, broad fences, where it creates a dense screen. Vines easily climb trees—a popular treatment in England—but are too vigorous for all but large species, such as oaks and maples. An excellent choice for a hard-to-plant north-facing surface, and urban and seaside gardens, this vine initially may need pinning to attach to vertical surfaces but then ascends without assistance.

HOW TO GROW: Climbing hydrangea is famous for starting slowly, but once its roots are established, it grows rapidly (feeding with a balanced organic fertilizer in spring will help spur growth). Plants do well in full sun or light shade—choose shade in warm regions—and prefer soil that is slightly acid, rich in organic matter, and moist but not soggy. Mulch annually with compost. If necessary, prune vines in late winter or early spring to control size and outward-growing stems.

CULTIVARS & RELATED SPECIES: A Himalayan native, *H. anomala* (Zone

5) also has white flowers but more coarsely toothed leaves and grows to 35'. From Chile and Argentina, *H. serratifolia* (Zone 8) has leathery evergreen foliage and inconspicuous white flowers. Climbing hydrangea is sometimes confused with Japanese climbing hydrangea (*Schizophragma hydrangeoides*, see page 92) and with Southeast climbing hydrangea or wood vamp (*Decumaria barbara*), a native American vine that flowers about a month earlier than climbing hydrangea and is hardy only to Zone 7.

Ipomoea alba

MOONFLOWER
Belle de nuit

Moonflower, the nighttime version of the morning glory, climbs by twining. Attractive large leaves provide a backdrop for this vine's stunning 6"-wide, pure white flowers (sometimes moonflowers are faintly banded with green). The sweetly fragrant flowers, which are magnets for nocturnal moths, open in early evening and last only until the next morning (on overcast days, the blooms will remain open far longer).

NATIVE HABITAT: American tropics and subtropics

USDA HARDINESS ZONE: 8

HABIT & GARDEN USE: Grown primarily for their nighttime blooms, by day moonflower vine's dense heart-

Fast-growing moonflower bears large, fragrant white blossoms that open at night.

shaped leaves create a handsome screen. Vines reach a height of 15' or more when treated as annuals; beginning in summer, they are covered with blossoms every night until the vines are killed by frost. Many gardeners combine moonflowers and morning glories (*I. tricolor*, see page 75) on a single trellis for 24 hours of bloom. Moonflower is traditionally grown on porches, where its fragrance and beauty can be enjoyed on summer evenings, and it also grows well in containers.

HOW TO GROW: Moonflowers need warmth, average garden soil that drains well, full sun or, in hot regions, midday shade, and strings, wires, or a trellis where its prickly stems can twine. In frost-free regions, sow directly outdoors. Moonflower seeds germinate with ease if soaked overnight in warm water or nicked with a file. In colder areas, begin seeds indoors, 6 to 8 weeks before the last frost, using individual pots. Transplant moonflower vines after the danger of frost has passed; when the ground has warmed fully, mulch vines with compost. For more vigorous growth, feed young moonflower vines every 3 weeks with a low-nitrogen, organic fertilizer. To control aphids, use a strong spray of water from a hose.

CULTIVARS & RELATED SPECIES: 'Giant White' bears especially large flowers.

Cypress vine has featherlike leaves.

Ipomoea quamoclit

CYPRESS VINE
Indian pink, star climber, star-glory

An under-appreciated species and member of a large genus that includes morning glories and moon-flowers, cypress vine climbs by twining. The featherlike dark green leaves would be reason enough to grow this vine, so the 1½" scarlet, trumpetlike blossoms that flare into five-point stars (the anthers are tipped with contrasting white pollen) are icing on the garden cake. Vines grow to 20'. Cypress vine flowers all summer, but the blooms, which last only a day, close when the sun comes out. Vines are extremely tender and completely intolerant of frost.

NATIVE HABITAT: American tropics
USDA HARDINESS ZONE: Annual in all zones

HABIT & GARDEN USE: Cypress vine climbs quickly and easily on strings, stakes, posts, wires, or trellises, or will clamber over a garden wall. It is pretty when grown in hanging containers or flower boxes, where its graceful stems can cascade. A good bloomer in partial shade, its delicate foliage creates an airy rather than a dense screen.

HOW TO GROW: Cypress vine needs good but not excessively rich garden soil, warmth, and plenty of water during summer heat. It does best in a sunny or partially shaded location that is sheltered from the wind. Good drainage is essential. Plants can be killed by temperatures in the mid-30s. Direct-sow after all danger of frost has passed, or begin plants indoors 6 weeks before the frost-free date.

CULTIVARS & RELATED SPECIES: 'Cardinalis' has brilliant red blooms, and 'Alba' bears white flowers. The blossoms of cardinal climber (*I. × sloteri*, Zone 9) are similar to cypress vine's.

Ipomoea tricolor

MORNING GLORY

Perhaps the most commonly grown of all tender vines, beloved for their beautiful 5-petaled trumpetlike flowers, morning glories have been garden stars for generations. The 4" blossoms fade in the afternoon—hence the common name—but are replaced the next morning with new flowers. Usually cultivated as an annual vine, morning glory is a short-lived perennial that climbs by twining.

NATIVE HABITAT: Mexico and Central America

USDA HARDINESS ZONE: 9

HABIT & GARDEN USE: Grown in the garden or in containers, morning glories are a fine choice for fences, trellises, wires, strings, posts, tepees, or arbors. The 5" heart-shaped medium-green leaves create a dense screen, and the vine, which grows to 15' and more, is a fine groundcover. Flowering begins in midsummer and lasts until plants are killed by frost. Many gardeners combine morning glories and night-flowering moonflowers (*I. alba*, see page 72) on a single trellis for 24 hours of bloom.

HOW TO GROW: Grow undemanding morning glories in a warm, sunny location and in light garden soil that drains well—tolerant of poor soil and moderate drought, these vines won't put up with soggy, heavy soil. Morn-

Morning glory creates a dense screen.

ing glories grow so fast that they can be sown directly outdoors after the last frost in all gardens except those with extremely short growing seasons. For an earlier start, begin seeds indoors, 4 weeks before the frost-free date, in individual pots, transplanting outdoors when the danger of frost has passed. To encourage vigorous growth, feed young plants once or twice with a low-nitrogen organic fertilizer. Pinch back stems to encourage

bushiness and to guide growth.
CULTIVARS & RELATED SPECIES:
Morning glory flower colors include white, blue, pink, red, magenta, maroon, and all shades between, as well as bicolored types. Among the best cultivars are 'Blue Dawn', 'Heavenly Blue', 'Heavenly Blue Improved' (extremely large blooms), 'Pearly Gates' (marbled white and blue), 'Crimson Rambler' (crimson with white throats), 'Wedding Bells' (pink-lavender), and 'Blue Star' (sky blue striped with dark blue).

I. nil and I. purpurea, which are also known as morning glory, are annual vines similar in appearance and culture to I. tricolor. Popular I. nil cultivars include 'Scarlett O'Hara' (red), 'Chocolate' (brown), and the 'Early Call' hybrids, which were bred for areas with short growing seasons. I. × imperialis, the imperial Japanese morning glory, is a showy I. nil hybrid known for its extremely large, double flowers that come in a huge range of colors. Good I. purpurea cultivars are 'Alba' (white), 'Kniola's Purple-Black', and 'Violacea', which has double purple blooms.

Wild sweet potato vine (I. pandurata) is a native American perennial twiner hardy to Zone 7 that has white flowers with purple throats; it is a rampant grower in some regions. Another cousin of morning glory, sweet potato vine (I. batatas), is a tender perennial grown for its dark purple, lobed leaves and cascading habit.

Jasminum species

JASMINE
Jessamine

Most jasmines have clusters of star-like tubular white, yellow, or pink flowers that are extremely fragrant. Blooming times vary, but the most frequently cultivated species flower in summer. Many experts consider jasmines to be the best of all fragrant plants. However, two species, Brazilian jasmine (*J. dichotomum*) and Gold Coast jasmine (*J. azoricum*), have become invasive in southern Florida and should not be planted outdoors by tropical and subtropical gardeners.
NATIVE HABITAT: Tropics and subtropics worldwide
USDA HARDINESS ZONES: 8 to 11
HABIT & GARDEN USE: Twining vines that can be grown in pots or hanging containers as well as in the garden, jasmines should be located where you can enjoy their unsurpassed fragrance. Young plants may need tying in order to climb.
HOW TO GROW: Jasmines prefer full sun or partial shade and well-drained, light soil that has been enriched with organic matter. Feed monthly during the growing season with a balanced organic fertilizer, and make sure that the soil remains moist but not soggy. Prune spring bloomers after they flower, summer bloomers in late winter. Gardeners in colder regions can

grow jasmines in containers and over-winter them indoors in a sunny location. Most species bloom only when the days are short and the nights are cool (60°F or lower).

SPECIES & CULTIVARS: Poet's or common jasmine (*J. officinale*), a vigorous vine—up to 35' in frost-free regions, 8' in cooler locations—has semi-evergreen leaves and clusters of white flowers that appear in early summer. Hardy to Zone 7, its fragrance is especially potent in the evening. 'Aureovariegatum' has variegated foliage; the flowers of 'Affine' are larger than the species', white inside, and pink outside.

Winter jasmine

The plant known as winter, Chinese, or pink jasmine (*J. polyanthum*, Zones 8 to 9) blooms in February in very warm regions or in late spring in cooler areas. The 20' evergreen vine bears large clusters of strongly scented 1" flowers that are white on the inside and streaked with pink or red on the outside. The vine commonly known as royal, Confederate, star, windmill, angel hair, or angel wing jasmine (*J. laurifolium* f. *nitidum*, Zone 8) has glossy dark green foliage and small clusters of 2"-wide pinwheel-like flowers, white on the inside and streaked with purple-pink on the outside. A superb container plant, it grows to about 10'.

Spanish, royal, or Catalonian jasmine (*J. officinale* f. *grandiflorum*, Zone 10) grows to 10', and has very fragrant white flowers from summer through autumn and semi-evergreen foliage.

Sometimes confused with true jasmines are Confederate jasmine (*Trachelospermum jasminoides*, see page 98) and Carolina jessamine (*Gelsemium sempervirens*, see page 69).

Lablab purpureus

HYACINTH BEAN
Lubia bean, dolichos bean, Indian bean, Egyptian bean

A tender short-lived perennial herb, hyacinth bean is typically grown as an annual in U.S. gardens. Semi-evergreen in frost-free regions, it climbs by twining. This vine, which can grow 10' to 20' in one season, has attractive purple-green leaves that complement

Hyacinth bean

Because all parts of the plant are ornamental, the vines add beauty to the garden from spring until frost. Moreover, all parts of the plant—young leaves, flowers, pods, and seeds—are edible.

HOW TO GROW: Treat hyacinth bean as you would any annual food crop. Sow the seeds directly in the garden after the danger of frost is past and the soil has warmed. (For an earlier start, begin seeds indoors in individual pots, 4 weeks before the transplant date.) Full sun and average garden soil that is well drained and amended with organic matter are ideal conditions, but this bean can put up with much less, including poor soil. Do not use high-nitrogen fertilizers, which will produce foliage at the expense of flowers.

CULTIVARS & RELATED SPECIES: 'Alba' and 'Giganteus' bear white flowers; 'Ruby Moon' has reddish flowers. Long-day, short-day, and day-neutral cultivars are available.

the spikes of small, fragrant, dark purple, sweet-pealike flowers that appear in summer. The flowers are followed by highly ornamental shiny, red-maroon 5" seed pods.

NATIVE HABITAT: Tropical Africa

USDA HARDINESS ZONE: 9

HABIT & GARDEN USE: At Thomas Jefferson's Monticello, hyacinth beans are grown on large trellises, but they will climb just about anything—wires, strings, poles, lattices, fences, arbors, trees, and brush. These vines grow quickly and create a dense screen; they also thrive in containers set on decks or patios.

Lagenaria siceraria

BOTTLE GOURD

White-flowered gourd, calabash gourd, Hercules' club, sugar trough gourd, dipper, trumpet gourd

Bottle gourd is a tender annual vine in the squash family (Cucurbitaceae) that ascends by twining its tendrils around any available support. Solitary 5-petaled white male flowers that open in the late afternoon and wilt in the morning sun and variously shaped green and yellow-green gourds are the assets of this fast-growing vine (the female flowers, white and bell-shaped, are smaller than the male blossoms). The slightly toothed medium green leaves, halfway between round and heart-shaped, have a rough texture, reminiscent of the foliage of other members of the squash family. The blossoms are slightly fragrant.

NATIVE HABITAT: Naturalized worldwide in pantropical regions

USDA HARDINESS ZONE: Annual in all zones

HABIT & GARDEN USE: Vines can reach 30' in one season and look their best on trellises or other supports where the fruits can hang down and be admired. Although typically used to make tools or other implements (thus common names like "sugar trough" and "dipper"), bottle gourds are edible. Harvest when the fruits are still young and tender, and prepare them as you would summer squash. Bottle gourds are commonly dried and turned into birdhouses.

HOW TO GROW: Bottle gourds need a long growing season. Sow seeds indoors at least 4 weeks before the last frost, using individual peat pots. Transplant, taking care not to disturb the roots, only after the ground has warmed and all danger of frost is well past. Choose a warm location that receives full sun (or partial shade in very hot regions) and is sheltered from strong winds; mulch plants after the soil has warmed. The soil, which must drain well, should contain plenty of humus. Be sure that plants receive moisture throughout the growing season, and pinch back stems to promote bushiness and flowering.

CULTIVARS & RELATED SPECIES: There are many cultivated variants, differing in the size and shape of the fruits. The luffa or dishcloth gourd (*Luffa cylindrica*) has white-to-yellow flowers and cucumber-shaped fruits. The vine known as snake gourd, serpent gourd, viper gourd, and club gourd (*Trichosanthes cucumerina* var. *anguina*) has white flowers and long, twisted fruits that turn orange when ripe. All are frost-tender.

Lapageria rosea

CHILEAN BELLFLOWER
Chile bells, copihue

Bellflower is a tender woody perennial that is evergreen in frost-free regions and climbs by its twining stems. Dark green leathery oval leaves accent the elegant, waxy rose-red bell-shaped flowers of this vine. Each narrow 3"-long bloom, which has overlapping petals and may be slightly marked with white, hangs down from its wiry stem, nodding in even the slightest breeze. Flowering

Chilean bellflower

begins in early summer and lasts into autumn. Vines reach from 10' to 25'.

NATIVE HABITAT: Argentina and southern Chile

USDA HARDINESS ZONES: 9 to 10

HABIT & GARDEN USE: These magnificent vines will grow on walls or trellises, or clamber overhead, where the pendulous flowers are more easily seen and the open foliage permits some light to filter through. A popular vine for greenhouse culture, Chilean bellflower is also a good choice for container growth, especially in cold regions where it can be overwintered indoors. Its flowers are long-lasting additions to bouquets.

HOW TO GROW: Cool but not cold growing conditions, high humidity, and summer shade are essential for this vine to flourish. Plant in a light, moisture-retentive soil that is rich in organic matter and has an acid pH

(6.5 or slightly lower). Mulch with compost and feed in fall and spring with a balanced organic fertilizer. Chilean bellflower needs plenty of water while growing actively. Prune in early spring to shape growth or remove deadwood.

CULTIVARS & RELATED SPECIES: Choices include var. *Albiflora* (white), 'Beatrice Anderson' (deep red), 'Nash Court' (pink flecked with rose), 'Penheale' (deep red), and 'Superba' (crimson). Don't confuse Chilean bellflower with Chilean glory flower (*Eccremocarpus scaber*, see page 67).

Lathyrus odoratus

SWEET PEA

Growing to about 6', sweet peas are beloved by generations of gardeners for their clusters of extraordinarily fragrant, showy flowers, which are purple in the species but are now available in a huge assortment of other colors and bicolors. These vines grow quickly, so gardeners can expect flowers in early summer, about 10 weeks after the seeds germinate. Like garden peas, sweet peas use tendrils to climb.

NATIVE HABITAT: Crete, Italy, and Sicily

USDA HARDINESS ZONE: Annual in all zones

HABIT & GARDEN USE: Sweet peas are so popular that they are the sub-

Generations of gardeners have loved sweet peas for their showy, fragrant flowers.

ject of entire books and the focus of plant societies throughout the world; growing them is a competitive sport in England. They are superb cut flowers. The winged stems need support, such as strings, tepees, or lattices, to which they can attach their tendrils; or allow plants to sprawl on the ground to form a colorful and fragrant ground cover. Sweet peas also grow well over shrubs, walls, or fences. (Dwarf cultivars, such as 'Bijou', 'Cupid', and 'Knee-Hi', lack tendrils).

HOW TO GROW: Damp and cool are the operative words for growing this annual successfully. Many seed catalogs group sweet peas by when they bloom: early-flowering types, bred for regions with mild winters, are planted in late summer and blossom in midwinter; spring-flowering sweet peas are sown either in early fall or late winter and bloom in spring; and summer flowering types, which are sown in late fall or spring, blossom in summer. (Gardeners in northern climates may want to get a headstart by sowing seeds indoors in individual peat pots.) Choose a sunny outdoor location that has deeply dug, moderately rich soil that has been generously amended with well-rotted manure. Mulch plants with compost and keep them evenly moist; feed with a balanced organic fertilizer when the first flower buds appear. Pinch back vines to encourage branching, and remove spent flowers regularly to prolong blooming.

CULTIVARS & RELATED SPECIES: Hundreds of cultivars are available in white, cream, red, scarlet, claret, rose, mauve, pink, blue, lavender and more, as well as striped, spotted, and bicolored varieties, on long, medium, or short stems. Among the most fragrant prize-winning cultivars are 'Corinne' (carmine and white), 'Memories' (rose-pink on white), 'Wiltshire Ripple' (white striped with claret), 'World's Children' (red and orange bicolor), 'Maggie May' (sky blue), and 'White Supreme'. Good sweet pea mixes, all fragrant, are 'Floral Tribute', 'Fragrantissima', and the heirloom 'Painted Lady'.

Two-flowered pea (*L. grandiflorus*) and the vine known as everlasting pea or perennial pea (*L. latifolius*) are two perennial members of the genus. Both have magenta-pink, pink, or white flowers and are not fragrant; they are hardy to Zones 4 to 5. Lord Ansom's blue pea (*L. nervosus*, Zones 6 to 7) is a short-lived perennial species that bears small fragrant purple-blue flowers.

Lonicera species

HONEYSUCKLE
Woodbine

Most honeysuckles grown in U.S. gardens are hardy woody vines that climb by twining. One widely planted honeysuckle, Japanese honeysuckle

(*L. japonica*), is extremely invasive in more than two dozen eastern and midwestern states and should not be planted. Native honeysuckles, such as coral honeysuckle (*L. sempervirens*), are a wiser choice. Honeysuckles bear pairs, whorls, or clusters of tubular, or trumpetlike, 2-lipped, 5-lobed flowers. Attractive to hummingbirds, bees, moths, and other wildlife, the blooms vary in color, from white and yellow to orange and red. The blossoms of many species are fragrant, typically opening in late spring and early summer; some species continue flowering into autumn. The vine's shiny red or black berries, which are popular with birds and other wildlife, are also ornamental. Most honeysuckles grow 15' or taller (some much taller); many species are evergreen or semi-evergeen in warm regions and deciduous in colder parts of their range.

NATIVE HABITAT: Asia

USDA HARDINESS ZONE: 3 and warmer, depending on the species

HABIT & GARDEN USE: Non-invasive forms of honeysuckle are ideal for covering arbors, bowers, trellises, pergolas, tree stumps, rocky outcrops, walls, and fences. They also make colorful groundcovers for a slope (they are frequently recommended for erosion control). Gardeners often espalier honeysuckles in climates where the vines are evergreen. Most species grow very quickly.

HOW TO GROW: Most honeysuckles

Coral honeysuckle

do well in either sun or part shade and in ordinary soil, but they prefer moist conditions (trumpet honeysuckle is drought-tolerant) and ground that has been enriched with compost or other organic matter. Cut back new plants by half to encourage branching. Honeysuckles need little care beyond some pruning of old wood and an annual mulching with compost. Additional fertilizer, especially high-nitrogen fertilizer, will produce lush foliage but reduce flowering. Flowers are produced on new wood, so prune vines in late winter or very early spring to control growth.

CULTIVARS & RELATED SPECIES: The common name "Scarlet trumpet honeysuckle" describes *L.* × *brownii* well. 'Dropmore Scarlet', which has red flowers, is the best-known cultivar; it blooms in midsummer and has a long flowering season (Zone 3). Western trumpet honeysuckle (*L. ciliosa*, Zone 5) is a summer-blooming American native with yellow and orange-red flowers.

Semi-evergreen goldflame or everblooming honeysuckle (*L.* × *heckrottii*) has showy fragrant blooms that are pinkish purple outside and yellow inside. These vines, which are weak-stemmed and hardy to Zone 5, grow to about 12'. 'Goldflame' has dark green foliage and purple and yellow flowers. Henry honeysuckle (*L. henryi*, Zone 4) has small purple-red to red blooms that open in summer, blue-black fruits, and semi-evergreen foliage. It grows as tall as 30'.

Giant Burmese honeysuckle (*L. hildebrandiana*, Zone 9) has glossy 5" oval leaves; in summer, it bears eye-catching 7", fragrant, cream-colored flowers that turn to yellow-orange. Its rope-sized woody vines can climb as high as 75'. A popular cultivar in southern California and similar climates, it requires plenty of space, strong support, and vigorous pruning.

Common honeysuckle or woodbine (*L. periclymenum*) is a shrubby vine with summer-blooming fragrant flowers, which are red-purple outside and yellow inside, and bright red fruits. Evergreen in mild-winter regions, it is deciduous elsewhere and hardy to Zone 4. There are many cultivated forms, including 'Aurea' (yellow variegated foliage), 'Berries Jubilee' (yellow), and 'Graham Thomas' (large white flowers that turn copper-yellow). Among the late Dutch honeysuckle types are 'Serotina' (purple and cream-colored flower), and 'Serpentine', which has leaves with blue undersides and mauve and cream flowers that appear in midsummer and autumn.

The trumpet, or coral, honeysuckle (*L. sempervirens*, Zone 3), native to the eastern U.S., is a fast-growing deciduous (evergreen in warm regions) climber (to 45') with striking orange-red and yellow flowers followed by bright red berries. It flowers best in full sun and is an excellent choice for gardens, although it has no scent. Vines bloom from spring through fall. Named cultivars include 'Magnifica' and 'Red Coral'/'Superba'.

L. tragophylla, a vigorous shrubby vine from China with very large, unscented white flowers that turn yellow, does well in shaded locations. It grows to 15' and is hardy to Zone 6.

Mandevilla splendens

MANDEVILLA

Although the sparsely foliated vine is attractive, it is the clusters of 4" trumpetlike flowers that open with blush-pink petals and slowly change to a

Mandevillas are good vines for small gardens, patios, terraces, and decks.

rich rose that are the main attraction. Blooms, which have 5 flaring lobes, are long lasting and may appear from spring into fall. Mandevilla has 6" oblong leathery foliage that is glossy and, in some cultivars, handsomely textured. Mandevillas are tuberous evergreen perennials. Sometimes referred to as "dipladenias," a holdover from their former botanical name, they climb by twining.

NATIVE HABITAT: Central and South American tropics

USDA HARDINESS ZONE: 10

HABIT & GARDEN USE: Because mandevillas are totally intolerant of cold, they are often cultivated in greenhouses, indoors, or outside in containers that are brought inside when the temperatures drop. They require a trellis for support, some-thing around which they can twine, and grow steadily to about 8' (they may reach two or three times as tall when grown in the ground in frost-free climates). Plants are rarely both-ered by insects or diseases and are ideal for small gardens, patios, ter-races, and decks. Tolerant of sea air, they are popular with coastal garden-ers in southern California and similar settings.

HOW TO GROW: Plant in fertile soil that is rich in humus. Whether in a large container or planted in the ground, mandevillas need soil that retains moisture and drains well. Locate them in an airy, sunny spot (with afternoon shade in hot, arid regions) and provide plenty of water during the heat of summer. Feed con-tainer plants with a balanced organic fertilizer applied at $\frac{1}{2}$ strength every 3 weeks during the spring and summer, and mist them frequently. Allow plants to dry out after flowering has stopped. Pinch stem tips to promote fuller growth; prune, if needed, in late winter.

CULTIVARS & RELATED SPECIES: 'Alice Du Pont' (*M.* × *amoena*, Zone 11) is the evergreen mandevilla most commonly found in nurseries. An exceptional hybrid, bright pink with darker rose and yellow at the throat, it blooms for 6 months and longer. Chilean jasmine (*M. laxa*, Zone 10) is a fragrant, deciduous species with ivory flowers and oval or heart-shaped leaves; more vigorous and hardy than *M. splendens*, it can be grown in Zone 8 with protection. M. sanderi 'Red Riding Hood' is a short evergreen vine with dark pinkish red blossoms with yellow throats (Zone 10).

Manettia luteorubra

FIRECRACKER VINE
**Twining firecracker,
Brazilian firecracker**

Firecracker vine is a tender evergreen twiner that features closely-

Grown in a container, firecracker vine provides a bright accent on a deck or patio.

leafed vines bearing 1" tubular flowers. The solitary, waxy blooms resemble lighted firecrackers—or Halloween candy corn, according to some—each orange-red with a yellow tip. Plants are nearly everblooming in frost-free locations; flowering typically occurs from late fall into spring indoors. Vines grow up to 10' (shorter in containers) and are covered with glossy oval leaves.

NATIVE HABITAT: American tropics

USDA HARDINESS ZONE: 10

HABIT & GARDEN USE: Firecracker vine, except in extremely warm climates, must be treated as an annual, or cultivated as a container plant and brought indoors during cool weather. Either way, let vines twine on wires or small lattices. Firecracker vines provide a bright accent on decks and patios, where children especially will be delighted by the red and yellow flowers.

HOW TO GROW: Firecracker vines, which should be planted in humus-rich soil that drains well, need warmth and protection from the wind. Choose a location with light shade outdoors, or bright light indoors. Water firecracker vine regularly while it is growing actively, but reduce water once flowering has ceased. Pruning is rarely required, but pinch back stems to encourage branching.

CULTIVARS & RELATED SPECIES: *M. cordifolia*, also known as firecracker vine, is similar to *M. luteorubra* and is also hardy only to Zone 10.

Menispermum canadense

MOONSEED
Yellow parilla

Moonseed is a woody dioecious vine—the male and female flowers are produced on separate plants—that climbs by twining. Evergreen in warmer climates, moonseed dies to the ground each winter in more northern regions but grows back rapidly each spring, reaching up to 15'. Plants have ivylike leaves, 4" across, and bloom throughout the summer. The clusters of small greenish yellow cup-shaped flowers are attractive but not showy. The black, grapelike fruits are poisonous, but moonseed roots are used medicinally as a tonic, for arthritis and other ailments. The common name comes from the shape of the grooved stones inside the fruits.

NATIVE HABITAT: Eastern North America

USDA HARDINESS ZONE: 5

HABIT & GARDEN USE: Because moonseed grows well in shade and on poor soil that is slightly wet, it is a fine choice for locations where most vines fail. Its dense, glossy foliage is useful for blanketing walls and wire fences, on banks for erosion control, or on rocky terrain—but plants need a support in order for the slender stems to twine upward. Remember, too, that both male and female plants are necessary in order to produce the attractive clusters of fruits. Vigorous, even aggressive, this vine belongs only in a large garden where it won't overwhelm other plants.

HOW TO GROW: Moonseed does best in moist, organically rich soil, but it is tolerant of almost all conditions, including wind, shade, and thin, wet ground. Vines spread quickly by underground rhizomes. Prune heavily in spring to control and shape growth, and don't drop the cuttings carelessly or put them in your compost, for they root easily whenever they touch soil. Be warned: Once out of bounds, moonseed is extremely difficult to rein in.

CULTIVARS & RELATED SPECIES: Asiatic moonseed (*M. davuricum*, Zone 4) is similar to *M. canadense* but slightly more hardy.

Passiflora caerulea

PASSION FLOWER

Blue passion flower, blue crown passion flower

There are more than 500 *Passiflora* species, many of which are vines or scandent shrubs originating in tropical regions throughout the world. Blue passion flower is a semi-evergreen vine that uses tendrils to climb. The complex, slightly fragrant, 4" flowers of this species are said to suggest the Passion of Christ: 10 petals represent the Apostles (minus Peter and Judas); the filaments of the corona are the crown of thorns; the 5 anthers represent Christ's five wounds; and the 3 styles symbolize the three nails. Vines can reach 25' and have varied, deep green lobed leaves. They flower from midsummer until autumn. The yellow-orange egg-like fruits develop only where the growing season is long. Edible but nearly flavorless in this species, the fruits detach from the vine when ripe.

NATIVE HABITAT: Brazil and Argentina

USDA HARDINESS ZONES: 7 to 8

HABIT & GARDEN USE: Blue passion flower is one of the hardiest *Passiflora* species and may survive in Zone 6 if planted in a warm, protected location and mulched heavily in late fall. Don't give up on vines that are winter-killed—new shoots likely will appear in the spring. More vigorous in warmer regions, where they tolerate heat and wind, these vines should be grown against a good-sized trellis or wire screen, so their flowers are accessible to insect and avian admirers as well as human ones. Gardeners in cold climates will do best if they cultivate passion flower in a large container, bring it indoors before the first frost, and over-winter it in a cool, well-lighted location.

HOW TO GROW: Passion flower vines will grow in the shade but only flower well when located in full sun. A moderately fertile soil is adequate, but it should have a near-neutral pH, be

Blue passion flower is one of the hardiest passifloras, and can grow quite tall.

deeply dug and rich in humus, and drain well. Plants need plenty of water when growing and flowering, and also benefit from a semiannual mulching with compost and well-rotted manure. (Container plants should be fed monthly with a balanced organic fertilizer applied at ½ strength; allow the soil to dry out during the plant's dormancy.) Vines grow rapidly and easily become tangled, making regular thinning necessary. Blossoms are produced on new growth, so prune vigorously in late winter or early spring.

CULTIVARS & RELATED SPECIES: 'Constance Eliott' has ivory flowers; 'Grandiflora' bears 6" blossoms.

The native maypop (*P. incarnata*) is hardy to Zone 6 and has edible yellow fruits. Also known as wild passion flower, apricot vine, and May apple, maypop produces pale lavender flowers for up to 10 months in very warm regions.

P. × *alato-caerulea*, a hybrid with good resistance to caterpillars, has large white to rose-pink flowers (Zone 9). 'Imperatrice Eugénie' has 6" blossoms. The species known as granadilla, purple granadilla, and passion fruit (*P. edulis*, Zone 10) is grown commercially for its fruits. There are many named cultivars, including 'Alice' and 'Red Giant', that have purple fruits.

Red passion flower, or red granadilla (*P. coccinea* , Zone 10), has 5" scarlet flowers and edible yellow-orange striped fruits. Another species also known as red passion flower (*P. vitifolia*, Zone 10) has bold crimson flowers and grows to 20'.

Giant granadilla (*P. quadrangularis*, Zone 10) is the largest species, growing to 50' and bearing 5" mauve-pink flowers; 'Variegata' has leaves splashed with yellow.

Polygonum aubertii

SILVER LACE VINE
Silver fleece vine, fleece flower, China fleece vine

Silver lace vine has attractive light green leaves with wavy edges, but its best characteristic is the 6" upswept sprays of fragrant white or greenish white flowers, a welcome sight in midsummer and fall when few other woody plants bloom (in warm regions, flowering may begin as early as June). It is an extremely fast-growing semi-evergreen vine that twines its wiry stems around supports in order to climb. Plants can stand up to city and coastal conditions, require little attention, and are unbothered by pests or diseases.

NATIVE HABITAT: China, Tibet, and Russia

USDA HARDINESS ZONE: 4

HABIT & GARDEN USE: Although too vigorous for extremely small gardens—it grows 15' to 30' in a single season—silver lace vine is a superb and underplanted climber. It is useful as a cover trailing over unsightly rocks and stumps (few vines are better on a chain link fence) but looks its best when allowed to cascade from walls, fences, arbors, and pergolas. A born rambler, this vine can withstand rough treatment. If killed to the ground by the cold, it recovers and blooms the following season. Although a twiner, silver lace vine's long, heavy stems may need to be tied to their support.

HOW TO GROW: Silver lace vine does well in part shade, even in poor and dry soil, but it prefers full sun and organically rich ground that retains moisture but is not soggy. Still, this is a climber that requires more curbing than encouragement. Because it flowers on new wood, many gardeners cut it to the ground in late winter to control its size. Established plants don't need fertilizer, but should be mulched with compost each fall.

CULTIVARS & RELATED SPECIES: No cultivars of this superb vine have been introduced. The species known as Russian vine and bokara vine (*P. baldschuanicum*, Zone 4) is another vigorous climber but has pinkish white flower clusters and heart-shaped leaves.

Purple bell vine

Rhodochiton atrosanguineum

PURPLE BELL VINE

Purple bell vine climbs by twining its slender stems and the stalks, or petioles, of its semi-evergreen leaves. A tender perennial that is relatively new to the nursery trade, it can be cultivated as an annual in cold regions. Pur-

ple bell vine grows quickly but rarely ventures higher than 10'. Its real attraction, however, is not its diminutive size but its long-lasting 1" double bell-like (or lampshadelike) flowers, which are produced by the dozens and hang singly on thread-thin stems, rather like fuchsia flowers. Purple bell vine flowers develop over time: The upper, or first, bell is pinkish purple, while the second, which is blackish purple and suspended inside the first like a clapper, emerges as its seeds ripen. The 3" heart-shaped leaves are sometimes tinged with purple.

NATIVE HABITAT: Mexico

USDA HARDINESS ZONE: 9

HABIT & GARDEN USE: Because of its size, this summer-flowering climber is ideal for small gardens in frost-free parts of the country. Train it to twine around a small post, lattice, or strings where its unusual blooms can be admired, or grow it in a hanging container, window box, or pot. It is also a good species for climbing up shrubs or small trees. Northern growers can treat purple bell vine as an annual, or as a perennial, bringing it indoors in late autumn and overwintering it in a cool, bright location.

HOW TO GROW: Purple bell vine grows in sandy soil in the wild, but gardeners should add plenty of humus when planting this climber. In addition to light, well-draining soil, make sure plants get full sun (partial shade in hot regions), plenty of warmth, and protection from the wind. Vines begun from seed usually flower the first year if sown early. In cold regions, start seeds about 2 months before the normal transplant date. Do not transplant until all danger of frost has past and temperatures are above 55°F. Container plants should be fed every 4 weeks with a balanced organic fertilizer applied at ½ strength. No pruning is necessary, but pinch back shoots to increase fullness.

CULTIVARS & RELATED SPECIES: None are available.

Rosa species

CLIMBING ROSE

See "Climbing Roses," page 44.

Schizophragma hydrangeoides

JAPANESE HYDRANGEA VINE

A cousin of the better-known climbing hydrangea (*Hydrangea petiolaris*, see page 71), this deciduous climber ascends with adhesive aerial roots on its stems. Although mature vines, which grow to 35', provide a handsome foliage cover (the deep green leaves are opposite, oval-shaped, and toothed), the 8" flower clusters are the main attraction. Each cream-white flower cluster is made up of scores of tiny fertile blossoms surrounded by much larger, sterile, heart-shaped sepals. Vines bloom in midsummer.

'Roseum' Japanese hydrangea vine

NATIVE HABITAT: Japan and Korea
USDA HARDINESS ZONE: 6
HABIT & GARDEN USE: Japanese hydrangea vine flowers best in sun but can be planted on a north wall, one of the few vines that tolerates considerable shade. Beautiful when allowed to climb a tree, it is also a good vine for scaling walls and buildings. It is especially striking when grown against a stone wall. Plants may be hardy in Zone 5 in a protected location and mulched in fall.
HOW TO GROW: Locate in a partially shaded spot in warm regions. Culture is similar to that of climbing hydrangea (see page 71).
CULTIVARS & RELATED SPECIES: 'Moonlight' has white blossoms and striking blue-green foliage; 'Roseum' has rose-pink tinted flowers. *S. integrifolium* has even larger white flower clusters (12") and grows to 45'. It should be planted in partial shade (Zones 7 to 8).

Solandra maxima

CHALICE VINE

Golden chalice, copa de oro, cup of gold vine, trumpet plant

A climbing woody shrub, chalice vine is a semi-epiphyte—a plant that in the wild sometimes uses another plant for support but is not parasitic. The glossy oval evergreen leaves form a lovely backdrop for this vine's 8"-wide

Chalice vine

chalice-shaped flowers of golden yellow, striped inside with maroon. The blooms, which have ruffled edges and are strongly scented, are pale when they first open, darkening as they mature. The flowers are followed by red fruits.
NATIVE HABITAT: Mexico and tropical Central America
USDA HARDINESS ZONE: 10
HABIT & GARDEN USE: Tolerant of wind, fog, and salt spray, chalice vine blooms over a long period of time, beginning in autumn when the shorter days trigger the formation of buds. In warm regions, vines grow quickly, to 40', and are lovely when affixed to stone, brick, and stucco walls, or to pillars, arbors, or pergolas. Considered a leaner, chalice vine must be secured to vertical supports.
HOW TO GROW: Chalice vine needs full sun in coastal settings, partial shade in hot areas, warmth, humidity,

and moderately rich soil that drains well. (Or cultivate in containers in cold climates, moving plants indoors well before the first frost and placing them in a bright, cool location.) Keep plants well watered when they are growing actively; reduce water during the summer, when the plant rests. Mulch lightly with compost to retain moisture and keep roots cool. Plants bloom on the tips of new wood; prune long stems in late winter to control growth and promote flowering. **CULTIVARS & RELATED SPECIES:** Silver chalices (*S. guttata* and *S. grandiflora*) are similar to chalice vine; Gabriel's trumpet (*S. longiflora*) has white flowers.

Stephanotis floribunda

MADAGASCAR JASMINE
Floradora, bridal wreath, chaplet flower, wax flower

It is Madagascar jasmine's powerful fragrance that has made this vine famous. Unrelated to true jasmine, it is an evergreen shrub that climbs by twining. Lovely, too, are its waxen blooms of purest white—1"- to 2"-long funnels that end in 5 distinct lobes—and its dark green 5" leaves, thick, glossy foils for the clusters of flowers. The buds take their time to open: Flowering usually begins in June and continues throughout the summer. Blooms are long lasting, both on the vine and when cut. The small egg-shaped fruits may hang on the vine for as long as 2 years while their seeds ripen.

NATIVE HABITAT: Madagascar
USDA HARDINESS ZONE: 10
HABIT & GARDEN USE: A traditional ingredient of bridal bouquets and leis, Madagascar jasmine should be planted close to the house or outdoor living area so its scent can be enjoyed. Slow-growing in a container, Madagascar jasmine will climb 15' or more when planted in the ground. A superb plant for patio, deck, or portico, this vine should be set against a trellis, fence, or other support. In cool climates, it traditionally is grown in a pot and trained on a wire hoop. Plants are long-lived but may take several years before they flower for the first time.

HOW TO GROW: Give this vine full sun in the North—perhaps a bit of midday shade during the summer months—and filtered bright light in really hot regions. Madagascar jasmine needs plenty of warmth and moderate humidity, and prefers slightly acid, fertile soil that has been generously amended with humus. Mulch vines to retain moisture. In cold regions, container plants should be taken indoors well before the first frost and overwintered in a location that gets good light and has a temperature range between 50° and 60°F. Reduce watering in winter, when vines are resting. Mature Madagascar jasmine vines benefit from being fertilized during active growth; use a balanced organic fertilizer and apply at ½ strength. Flowers are produced on new shoots, so prune in late winter or early spring, before growth begins. **CULTIVARS & RELATED SPECIES:** None are available.

Tecomaria capensis

CAPE HONEYSUCKLE

Cape honeysuckle

A loose, rambling tropical evergreen "shrub with climbing tendencies," Cape honeysuckle has a mild inclination to twine its long shoots. It has compound leaves with shiny opposite, toothed leaflets and bears tight clusters of 2" funnel-shaped flowers—colored brilliant orange-scarlet—at its stem ends. It flowers in summer and into autumn. The flowers are followed by long narrow seedpods. Close to carefree, Cape honeysuckle is ideal for poor, sandy, or stony soil, where other plants rarely flourish.
NATIVE HABITAT: South Africa
USDA HARDINESS ZONES: 8 to 9
HABIT & GARDEN USE: Moderately vigorous, extending about 20', this quasi-climber makes a fine cover for walls and trellises if tied to the vertical or horizontal structure. Cape honeysuckle is also used as an espalier, to blanket banks and steep slopes, or as a barrier plant. A good choice for container gardening, the vine is tolerant of heat, drought, wind, and salt air. Its roots send up new shoots; in congenial settings—sun and moist, fertile soil—it has the potential to be aggressive.
HOW TO GROW: All that's required to grow Cape honeysuckle is full sun—although plants will tolerate some shade—average soil, and good drainage. Avoid an extremely hot location. In cold regions, grow Cape honeysuckle in a large container and overwinter it indoors in a cool, bright location. Plants respond to moderate humidity, soil that has been enriched with humus, and regular watering, but once established, Cape honeysuckles are altogether undemanding. They may be winterkilled in marginally warm locations but will resprout in spring. Prune container plants in late winter or early spring to control growth; to rejuvenate a plant, cut to within 6" of the ground.

Black-eyed Susan vine is grown as a summer annual outdoors or as a houseplant.

CULTIVARS & RELATED SPECIES: 'Aurea' has gold flowers and lighter green foliage than the species'; 'Apricot' is a compact cultivar with orange blossoms; the flowers of 'Coccinea' are scarlet; those of 'Salmonea' range from pink to orange.

Thunbergia alata

BLACK-EYED SUSAN VINE

Black-eyed Susie, clock vine

A fast-growing tender herbaceous perennial, black-eyed Susan vine is grown as a summer annual in both temperate and tropical regions. It climbs by twining. "Daisies on a vine" is a common description of this agreeable plant, with its masses of single white, buff, yellow, or orange flowers up to 2"

across, each with 5 flaring lobes and a dark purple-black throat that, from a distance, mimics a daisy's eye. Flowers appear from summer into fall and are backed by opposite pairs of arrow-shaped leaves that are slightly hairy.

NATIVE HABITAT: Tropical Africa

USDA HARDINESS ZONE: 9

HABIT & GARDEN USE: Black-eyed Susan vine will succeed not only in the garden, where it is superb for covering trellises, lattices, arches, and low walls (black-eyed Susan vine on a picket fence is a classic combination), but also in containers, pots, hanging baskets, and window boxes, and as a houseplant. Its winged stems grow as long as 8' but are easily controlled by pruning. Dense foliage and a profusion of flowers make this rambling twiner useful for covering banks or rocky terrain, or for obscuring an eyesore.

HOW TO GROW: Grow black-eyed Susan vine in pots or plant directly in the garden. In frost-free areas, sow seeds direct in fall or spring; in cold regions, start seeds in individual pots indoors, 6 to 8 weeks before the last frost. Plants normally bloom their first year. Black-eyed Susan vines do not like excessive heat, but need a sunny location in the cool North, partial shade in the South. Shield them from strong winds. Plant in light, moist soil that is rich in humus and drains well. Unless soil is extremely poor, do not fertilize. Mulch plants in marginally warm climates to help them overwinter. Young vines may need tying to their support; pruning is rarely required. Gardeners who cultivate black-eyed Susan vines as perennials often cut plants back to 6" from the ground to rejuvenate them. Container plants can be overwintered indoors.

CULTIVARS & RELATED SPECIES: 'Susy Mixed' bears flowers of yellow, orange, or white, some with a dark throat, some without; 'Angel Wings' is slightly fragrant.

Sweet clock vine (*T. fragrans*, Zone 10), another tender perennial, has fragrant flowers. Another South African, orange clock vine (*T. gregorii*, Zone 9) grows to 15' or more and has toothed leaves and flaring orange blooms. In warm regions, it blooms as long as 10 months, but it flowers only during the summer months in colder climates.

Thunbergia grandiflora

BENGAL CLOCK VINE
Blue clock vine, Indian sky flower, sky flower, blue sky vine, blue trumpet vine

Vines with choice blue flowers are rare, but this species produces them by the dozens: drooping clusters of showy, flaring tubular blooms, each 3" across and painted the color of the sky with a pale yellow throat. Bengal clock vine—the clock in the name comes from its habit of twining clockwise—is a tender evergreen perennial that climbs 20' to 30'. It flowers in midsummer in northern regions, or fall through spring in frost-free climates. Vines bear lush 8" oval leaves that will create a dense screen.

NATIVE HABITAT: India

USDA HARDINESS ZONES: 8 to 9

HABIT & GARDEN USE: Bengal clock vine possesses the same virtues as its cousin, black-eyed Susan vine (see page 96). It is a fine plant for garden or container (where it requires pinching back to control its growth and overwintering indoors). Growth is vigorous once plants are established, making this woody twiner a fine choice for covering an arbor, pergola, bathhouse, or large lattice. It creates full shade when used overhead.

HOW TO GROW: Bengal clock vine prefers partial shade, especially in hot regions, and needs plenty of moisture. Be sure to water deeply at the first sign of wilting. Its culture is similar to that of black-eyed Susan vine (see page 96).

CULTIVARS & RELATED SPECIES: 'Alba' has white flowers with yellow throats.

Trachelospermum jasminoides

CONFEDERATE JASMINE
Star jasmine

Neither a true jasmine nor a native of the Confederate states, Confederate jasmine is valued for its clusters of white, intensely fragrant star-shaped flowers, which twist slightly and open in the late spring and early summer. A rambling tender perennial with milky sap, Confederate jasmine has glossy, evergreen, lance-shaped foliage with marked veins and climbs by twining.

NATIVE HABITAT: China

USDA HARDINESS ZONE: 8

HABIT & GARDEN USE: Widely planted in warm parts of the country, Confederate jasmine is a tough plant that withstands drought, heat, and wind. Established vines grow to 20' but are slow to get started and attach themselves to supports in a half-hearted manner; tying is necessary to ensure they grow up rather than out. A good

Confederate jasmine, a faux jasmine, is a tough, boldly-scented sprawler.

container plant for gardeners north of the Mason-Dixon line, this sprawler also makes a fine groundcover for difficult locations, such as steep banks. Plant it against a pillar, fence, or lattice, but, no matter how you train it, locate it where you can enjoy its scent.

HOW TO GROW: Give Confederate jasmine full sun in northern gardens, partial shade in warm regions, a moderately fertile soil amended with humus, even moisture, and a compost mulch in late spring and again in autumn. Container-grown vines must be pinched back to control growth and fed monthly with a balanced organic fertilizer applied at $1/2$ strength. Plants overwintered indoors should be set in a bright, cool location; allow soil to dry between watering and do not fertilize. This faux jasmine blooms on old wood, so prune stems immediately after flowering ceases to shape or limit growth.

CULTIVARS & RELATED SPECIES: 'Japonicum' has leaves veined with white; 'Variegatum' has green and white variegated leaves; 'Minimum' is a dwarf cultivar; rugged 'Madison' is hardy to Zone 7. *T. asiaticum*, from Japan and Korea, has pale yellow flowers and is most fragrant at dusk (Zone 7). Climbing dogbane (*T. difforme*, Zone 6) is a deciduous species from the southeastern U.S.; it bears clusters of fragrant greenish yellow flowers but is rarely cultivated.

Tropaeolum majus

NASTURTIUM
Garden nasturtium, climbing nasturtium, Indian cress

The spurred, 5-petaled, slightly scented flowers of nasturtium—in shades of cream, yellow, orange, red, and bicolors—have been loved by gardeners for centuries. There are single, semi-double, and double-flowered cultivars as well. Fine, too, are the species' round leaves, which are held on long stems that attach to the center of the leaf and are often described as looking like lily pads. This species ascends by grasping with its twining petioles, or leaf stems. Frost tender, nasturtiums bloom from summer into fall; plants will self-seed in warm climates and have escaped into the wild in coastal California and similar environments.

NATIVE HABITAT: Highlands of Central and South America

USDA HARDINESS ZONE: Annual in all zones

HABIT & GARDEN USE: Depending on the cultivar, vines grow up to 8' and are at home on trellises, strings, wires, and fences, where their foliage will create a dense screen; nasturtiums also make fine groundcovers. If you want a nasturtium that climbs, avoid "dwarf" or "mounding" types, which are the sort most widely sold (these types are useful for growing in pots, tubs, hanging baskets, and window boxes). Nasturtiums are often combined with other climbers and are long lasting as cut flowers (rather than a single bloom, cut a long stem that has many unopened buds). All above-ground parts of this species—flowers, foliage, and seed pods—are edible.

HOW TO GROW: One of the easiest annuals to grow, nasturtium should be sown directly outdoors as soon as the soil begins to warm, about a week before the frost-fee date in cold climates; in warm climates, sow seeds in autumn or very early spring. Seedlings don't always transplant well, but northern gardeners still may want to begin indoors, planting in individual containers about 4 weeks before the last frost.

Outdoors, locate nasturtiums in full sun, especially in the North; heavy shade will limit flowering. Although this annual prefers sun, it resents hot temperatures. Use average, even infertile, soil—high fertility will produce leaves rather than flowers—that is light and drains well. One of the rare garden plants that prefers sandy soil, nasturtium may need help attaching to supports. Water during prolonged periods without rain or if leaves begin to wilt. No pruning is necessary but pinch stem tips to increase branching. If plants are bothered by aphids, hose them with a strong spray of water.

CULTIVARS & RELATED SPECIES: Dozens of new cultivars are released every year, the majority of which are dwarf or mounding types. Climbing cultivars include 'Park's Fragrant Giants' (mixed colors), 'Fordhook Favorites' (mixed colors), 'Variegatum' (variegated leaves, orange/red flowers), 'Climbing Hybrid Improved' (mixed colors), 'Moonlight' (pale yellow), and 'Jung's Giant Climbing' (mixed colors).

The vine known as flame flower, Scottish flame flower, or flame nasturtium (*T. speciosum*, Zone 7) is a 10' perennial cousin of the nasturtium. It has brilliant red flowers with notched petals, lobed leaves, and attractive bright blue fruits; difficult to establish, it likes cool, moist conditions during the growing season. *T. tuberosum* and *T. tricolorum*, natives of Chile that are hardy to Zone 8, also are perennial species. The former has red and orange flowers and grows to 8'; 'Ken Aslett' has orange blooms. *T. tricolorum* has orange-red flowers rimmed in black with yellow petals.

Tropaeolum peregrinum

CANARY CREEPER
Canarybird vine

Orchidlike, 1", canary-yellow flowers with unusual fringed and frilled petals that look like the wings of a bird, and gray-green, deeply lobed, upturning

Canary creeper is the perfect accent for a patch of purple salvias.

leaves, reminiscent of a fig tree's, are two reasons that this underplanted species belongs in American gardens. Canary creeper is most often cultivated as a half-hardy annual; it uses twining petioles, which are touch-sensitive, or thigmotropic, to ascend. Plants, which can grow 10' in a single season, bloom from early summer into autumn.

NATIVE HABITAT: Andes Mountains

USDA HARDINESS ZONE: 9

HABIT & GARDEN USE: Use as with nasturtium (*Tropaeolum majus*, above). Canary creeper is an especially fine vine for wandering over and through other vines, shrubs, and small trees.

HOW TO GROW: Canary creeper tolerates partial shade and wants slightly richer, more moist soil than nasturtium does, but otherwise it can be cultivated as its better-known annual cousin is. For a headstart in cold regions—where this vine is best grown in a container—begin seeds indoors in individual pots 4 weeks before the frost-free date. Fertilize potted plants monthly with a balanced organic fertilizer applied at $\frac{1}{2}$ strength. Plants are a favorite stop for the cabbage butterfly. To control, handpick the caterpillars; for serious infestations, apply *Bacillus thuringiensis* (Bt). Cuttings made in late summer can be grown indoors in a sunny window throughout the winter.

CULTIVARS & RELATED SPECIES: No cultivars are available (for related species, see nasturtium, *Tropaeolum majus*, above).

Wisteria species

WISTERIA

Members of the pea family, wisteria species differ from one another, but all are famous for their pendulous racemes—elongated clusters—of flowers. There is a wide variety of colors, including pink, mauve, rose, blue, lavender, violet, and white; all species are fragrant. Wisteria foliage, which consists of pinnate, or compound, fernlike leaves, is also attractive. Named for University of Pennsylvania anatomy professor Caspar Wistar (1761-1818), wisterias are high-climbing deciduous woody twiners.

NATIVE HABITAT: East Asia and eastern North America.

USDA HARDINESS ZONES: 4 and warmer, depending on species (plants may survive in zones colder than those designated but may not flower).

HABIT & GARDEN USE: Wildly popular in the U.S., wisterias were born to decorate overhead supports, such as arbors, gateways, arches, and pergolas—any structures strong enough to support their vigorous twining stems and hanging flowers. This is the roofing vine par excellence. Wisterias are also effective wall plants, either free-ranging or as espaliers; plants are sometimes trained as standards. Mature vines can reach 40' or more and will develop trunk-like stems; most species flower in spring or early summer. Most wisterias are at least faintly fragrant and should be planted close to living areas, where their scent can be enjoyed.

HOW TO GROW: To make sure your wisteria will bloom—nonblooming is a frequent complaint—begin with a plant that has already flowered, has been grown from a cutting, or is budded or grafted, rather than a seedling. All wisterias like warmth and protection from strong winds. They do best in full sun and moist, moderately rich soil amended with humus, but they are not fussy plants. Good drainage is essential, but when they are in flower, wisteria vines need plenty of water.

Slightly acid soil is recommended; chlorosis may occur in vines planted in alkaline soil (yellow leaves with green veins is the telltale sign). Apply a balanced organic fertilizer; to reduce soil alkalinity, apply powdered sulfur or aluminum sulfate. Young plants benefit from monthly feedings of a balanced organic fertilizer, but established vines growing in healthy soil require little beyond a topdressing with compost once or twice a year (over-feeding with a high-nitrogen fertilizer will reduce flowering).

Pruning is important to control size and produce flower buds; pinch stem ends to promote branching. (For the special needs of this vine, which flowers on old wood, see "The Ways of Wisteria," page 31.)

CULTIVARS & RELATED SPECIES: The two most common garden species are Chinese and Japanese wis-

The long, dangling flowers of a venerable old Japanese wisteria adorn an arbor.

teria. Chinese wisteria (*W. sinensis*), the most frequently planted species, has become invasive throughout the eastern U.S. and is not recommended.

Japanese wisteria (*W. floribunda*, Zone 4) twines clockwise and grows to 35'. Its leaves are divided into 15 to 19 leaflets, and its violet or violet-blue fragrant flowers, which appear at the same time as the foliage in late spring to early summer, are held in racemes up to 24" long. Flowering begins at the top of the raceme and moves down toward the tip, prolonging the blooming season. The following cultivars are considered the best: 'Honbeni' or 'Rosea' (pink-lavender with a yellow blotch), 'Kuchibeni' (mauve-pink and purple), 'Lawrence' (blue-violet, very fragrant), 'Royal Purple' (purple with a yellow blotch), 'Shiro Noda' (white marked with yellow), and 'Violacea Plena' (violet, unique double flowers).

Kentucky wisteria (*W. macrostachys*, Zone 6) is a native species with 12" purple-lilac racemes with yellow markings; 'Aberville Blue' and 'Pondside Blue' have pale blue-violet flowers; 'Clara Mack' is white.

American wisteria (*W. frutescens*, Zone 5) is a 30' Southeast native bearing scented mauve flowers spotted with yellow. 'Nivea' has white flowers, 'Magnifica' clear blue.

Well-known cultivars of mysterious origin include 'Burford' (pale violet), 'Caroline' (pale violet with a yellow blotch), 'Formosa' (purple-violet with a yellow blotch), 'Lavender Lace', and 'Texas Purple'.

Vines are the stepchildren of seed companies and nurseries. Send for a half-dozen catalogs, however, and you're sure to find exactly the climber you're looking for. If uncommon species are your passion, be prepared to start from seed. The following list is divided into sources of plants and seeds.

PLANTS

AIMERS SEEDS
R.R. 3
Ilderton, Ontario
N0M 2A0 Canada
(905) 833-0282
Catalog $4
Also sells seeds

ARROWHEAD ALPINES
P.O. Box 857
Fowlerville, MI 48836
(517) 223-3581
Catalog $2
Also sells seeds

BUENA CREEK GARDENS
P.O. Box 2033
San Marcos, CA 92079
(760) 744-2810

BURNT RIDGE NURSERY & ORCHARDS
432 Burnt Ridge Road
Onalaska, WA 98570
(360) 985-2873
Catalog free

BUSSE GARDENS
5873 Oliver Avenue S.W.
Cokato, MN 55321-4229
(800) 544-3192
Catalog $2, refundable with order

CAMELLIA FOREST NURSERY
125 Carolina Forest
Chapel Hill, NC 27514
(919) 968-0504
Catalog $2

CANYON CREEK NURSERY
3527 Dry Creek Road
Oroville, CA 95965
(530) 533-2166
Catalog $2

CARROLL GARDENS
444 East Main Street
Westminster, MD 21157-5540
(410) 848-5422
Catalog $3, refundable with order

FORESTFARM
990 Tetherow Road
Williams, OR 97544
(541) 846-7269
Catalog $4

GREER GARDENS
1280 Goodpasture Island Road
Eugene OR 97401-1794
(541) 686-8266
Catalog $3

HERONSWOOD NURSERY, LTD.
7530 N.E. 288th Street
Kingston, WA 98346
(360) 297-4172
Catalog $5

MELLINGER'S, INC.
2310 West South Range Road
North Lima, OH 44452
(216) 549-9861
Catalog free
Also sells seeds

MILAEGER'S GARDENS
4838 Douglas Avenue
Racine, WI 53402-2498
(800) 669-9956

PLANTS OF THE WILD
P.O. Box 866
Tekoa, WA 99033
(509) 284-2848
Catalog $1

WHITE FLOWER FARM
P.O. Box 50
Litchfield, CT 06759
(800) 503-9624
Catalog free
www.whiteflowerfarm.
com

WOODLANDERS, INC.
1128 Colleton Avenue.
Aiken, SC 29801
(803) 648-7522
Catalog $2

SEEDS

**W. ATLEE BURPEE
& CO.**
300 Park Avenue
Warminster, PA 18974
(800) 888-1447
Catalog free
www.burpee.com

DEEP DIVERSITY
P.O. Box 15700
Santa Fe, NM 87505
(505) 438-8080
Catalog $6

THE FRAGRANT PATH
P.O. Box 328
Ft. Calhoun, NE 68023

**NORTHPLAN/
MOUNTAIN SEED**
P.O. Box 9107
Moscow, ID 83843-1607
(208) 882-8040
Seed list with SASE
email: norplan@
moscow.com

PARK SEED COMPANY
1 Parkton Avenue
Greenwood, SC 29647
(800) 845-3369
Catalog free

**THEODORE PAYNE
FOUNDATION**
10459 Tuxford Street
Sun Valley, CA 91352
(818) 768-1802
Catalog $2.50
email: theodorepayne@
juno.com

SBE SEED CO.
3421 Bream Street
Gautier, MS 39553
(800) 336-2064
Catalog $1, refundable
with order
email: seedman@
seedman.com
www.seedman.com

**SELECT SEEDS–
ANTIQUE FLOWERS**
180 Stickney Hill Road
Union, CT 06076
(860) 684-9310
Catalog $1

SILVERHILL SEEDS
P.O. Box 53108
Kenilworth
Cape Town 7745
South Africa
27 (21) 762-4245,
Catalog $2

**THOMPSON &
MORGAN**
P.O. Box 1308
Jackson, NJ 08527-0308
(800) 274-7333
Catalog free

Thanks to Dr. Samuel B. Jones, Jr., University of Georgia, for his help with native American vines; and to Ellen and J. Cary Davis, who first made me realize that flowers, like people, could rise to great heights.

—*K.D.C.*

ANDREW BUNTING
is the curator of the Scott Arboretum of Swarthmore College, in Swarthmore, Pennsylvania, and the owner of Fine Garden Creations, a garden design and installation business. Each year he teaches a six-week course on ornamental vines at Longwood Gardens, in Kennett Square, Pennsylvania.

KARAN DAVIS CUTLER
gardens on 15 acres in northern Vermont. An award-winning writer, newspaper columnist, and magazine editor, she is the author of *Burpee: The Complete Vegetable and Herb Gardener* (Macmillan,
1997) and is currently working on *The New England Gardener's Book of Lists*, forthcoming from Taylor Publishing in 1999.

KATHLEEN FISHER
a former newspaper reporter for *The Kansas City Star,* served as the editor/director for the American Horticultural Society for nine years. Now a freelance writer and editor—her current project is a book on medicinal herbs—she divides her time between gardens in Alexandria and Reedville, Virginia.

RICHARD HAWKE
has been the coordinator of Plant Evaluation Programs at Chicago Botanic Garden. He is the author of *Plant Evaluation Notes*, a periodic publication reporting the results of evaluation projects.

LEWIS HILL AND NANCY HILL
are widely known and respected garden writers living in northeastern Vermont. Authors of a dozen books and dozens of magazine articles, their latest title is *Pruning Made Easy* (Storey Books, 1997).

PETER LOEWER
is a writer, botanical artist, and photographer who gardens in the mountains of North Carolina. He has written many books on gardening and natural history. His latest book, *The Moonflower* (Peachtree, 1998), is for children.

ROBERT OSBORNE
is the owner of Corn Hill Nursery Ltd., a mail-order firm located in Petitcodiac, New Brunswick, Canada, where he grows hardy roses, ornamental flowers and shrubs, and fruits of all types. He is the author of *Hardy Roses* (Storey Books, 1991).

ILLUSTRATIONS

K. E. DAVIS
pages 7 and 93

ALAN & LINDA DETRICK
pages 6, 9, 78, and 103

CHRISTINE M. DOUGLAS
pages 14, 28, 41, 81, 89, and 95

DEREK FELL
pages 55, 59, 64, 65, 69, 86, and 101

SUSAN M. GLASCOCK
page 21

PAMELA HARPER
pages 49, 56, 71, 73, and 77

RICHARD HAWKE
page 36

HORTICULTURAL PHOTOGRAPHY
cover, pages 35, 53 (bottom), and 75

BOB HYLAND
pages 15, 19, 23, 53 (top), 74, 80, and 96

DENCY KANE
page 58

JERRY PAVIA
pages 1, 5, 11, 13, 24, 27, 33, 38, 45, 51, 54, 61, 63, 67, 70, 83, 85, 91, 92, and 98

INDEX

BROOKLYN BOTANIC GARDEN

21 ST-CENTURY GARDENING SERIES

THE SHADY BORDER
Knockout Plants that Light Up the Shadows

EASY COMPOST
The Secret to Great Soil and Spectacular Plants

TANTALIZING TOMATOES
Smart Tips & Tasty Picks for Gardeners Everywhere

GROWING FRUITS
Nature's Desserts

for further information please contact the

BROOKLYN BOTANIC GARDEN

1000 Washington Avenue

Brooklyn, New York 11225

(718) 622-4433 ext. 265 www.bbg.org

Watch our garden grow in your very own mailbox!

From Great Neck to Great Bend, Big River to Little Creek, over 20,000 people in all 50 states enjoy the bountiful benefits of membership in the **Brooklyn Botanic Garden** – including our renowned gardening publications.

Brooklyn Botanic Garden Membership

The splendor that makes the Brooklyn Botanic Garden one of the finest in the world can be a regular part of your life. BBG membership brings you subscriptions to some of the liveliest, best-researched, and most practical gardening publications anywhere – including the next entries in our acclaimed 21st-Century Gardening Series (currently published quarterly). BBG publications are written by expert gardeners and horticulturists, and have won prestigious *Quill and Trowel* awards for excellence in garden publishing.

SUBSCRIBER $35
(Library and Institution Rate $60)
- A full year of *21st-Century Gardening Series* handbooks
- A year's subscription to *Plants & Gardens News*
- Offerings of Signature Seeds, handbooks and videos
- Reciprocal privileges at botanical gardens across the country

Plants & Gardens News – practical t and suggestions from BBG experts.

FAMILY/DUAL $50
All benefits of SUBSCRIBER, plus
- Membership card for free admission for two adult members and their children under 16
- 10% discount at the Terrace Cafe & Garden Gift Shop
- Free parking for four visits
- Discounts on classes, trips and tours

SIGNATURE $125
All benefits of FAMILY, plus
- Your choice of a Signature Plant from our annual catalog of rare and unique shrubs, perennials and house plants
- 12 free parking passes
- A special BBG gift calendar

BBG Catalog – quarterly listing of classes, workshops and tours in the and abroad, all at a discount.

SPONSOR $300
All benefits of SIGNATURE, plus
- Your choice of <u>two</u> Signature Plants
- Four complimentary one-time guest passes
- 24 free parking passes
- Invitations to special receptions

GARDENING BOOKS FOR THE NEXT CENTURY
Brooklyn Botanic Garden's 21st-Century Gardening Series explore frontiers of ecological gardening - offering practical, step-by-step tips on creating environmentally sensitive and beautiful gardens for the 1990s and the new century.

Spring 1998
Please send in this form or contact BBG
for current membership information, higher levels and benefits.

21st-Century Gardening Series – the handbooks in this acclaimed library.

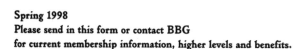